The 10 Principles Of Healing

1. **Principle of Perception.** Untangle yourself from the web of your addictive upbringing and heal your old mental pictures.

2. **Principle of Choice.** Realize that choices are available and choose the best.

3. **Principle of Vacuum.** Clear out addictive thoughts and feelings from your life so there will be room to receive healing and happiness.

4. **Principle of Optimism.** If you view your life in a more optimistic way, it will bring you joy and happiness.

5. **Principle of Expectation.** Create positive life conditions for yourself by expecting the best life has to offer.

6. **Principle of Harmony.** Establish more balance and harmony with yourself, your relationship and the world around you.

7. **Principle of Empowerment.** Empower yourself so that you become responsible for your life instead of being victimized by it.

8. **Principle of the Boomerang.** Project positive thoughts, feelings and actions that will return to enrich your life.

9. **Principle of Magnetism.** Attract people and events into your life that will mirror your healing self.

10. **Principle of the Inner Guru.** Heal yourself from the inside out instead of the outside in and find self-fulfillment on your inner journey.

Other Health Communications Publications
by Bryan E. Robinson

Work Addiction: Hidden Legacies of Adult Children.
**Soothing Moments: Daily Meditations for
Fast Track Living.**
Healograms: Healing Messages for Co-dependents.
Stressed Out? A Workbook for Balance and Serenity.

Heal Your Self-Esteem:

Recovery From Addictive Thinking

Bryan E. Robinson, Ph.D.

Health Communications, Inc.
Deerfield Beach, Florida

Bryan E. Robinson, Ph.D.
University of North Carolina at Charlotte
Charlotte, North Carolina

Library of Congress Cataloging-in-Publication Data

Robinson, Bryan E.
  Through healing eyes : recovery from addictive thinking / by Bryan
E. Robinson.
    p.   c.m.
  Includes bibliographical references.
  ISBN 1-55874-119-4
  1. Attitude (Psychology) 2. Thought and thinking. 3. Psychology,
Pathological. I. Title. II. Title: Addictive thinking.
  RC455.4.A86R63   1991
  616.86—dc20   90-5289
                                                                    CIP

©1991 Bryan E. Robinson
ISBN 1-55874-119-4

Publisher: Health Communications, Inc.
        3201 S.W. 15th Street
        Deerfield Beach, Florida 33442

DEDICATION

This book is dedicated to you and to me
as we change our lives by healing
our addictive thinking.

Autobiography In Five Short Chapters
by Portia Nelson

Chapter I
I walk down the street.
There is a deep hole in the sidewalk.
I fall in.
I am lost . . . I am helpless.
It isn't my fault.
It takes forever to find a way out.

Chapter II
I walk down the same street.
There is a deep hole in the sidewalk.
I pretend I don't see it.
I fall in again.
I can't believe I am in the same place.
But, it isn't my fault.
It still takes a long time to get out.

Chapter III
I walk down the same street.
There is a deep hole in the sidewalk.
I see it is there.
I still fall in . . . it's a habit.
My eyes are open.
I know where I am.
It is my fault.
I get out immediately.

Chapter IV
I walk down the same street.
There is a deep hole in the sidewalk.
I walk around it.

Chapter V
I walk down another street.

ACKNOWLEDGMENTS

I want to thank the many wonderful people in my life who helped make this book a reality. My special thanks to Jamey McCullers, Glenda Watson, Dr. Phyllis Post, Dr. Wanda Webb, Dr. Carol Flake, Bettie Dibrell, Belle Radenbaugh, Glenda Loftin and Bill Duane who read early drafts of the manuscript and offered me valuable and constructive feedback. Thanks to Marie Stilkind and Randy McKenzie for being the sounding board for the original conceptualization of the book and the title. Their help has been invaluable. Marie Stilkind was a steady and calm source of moral support. As always she has done a remarkable job on the copy-editing of the book and overseeing the process from beginning to end. My thanks go to Bettie Dibrell and Elaine Farthing for sharing Portia Nelson's poem. Dr. Robert Barret shared his model of co-dependency that I used in Chapter 11, as well as his ideas on co-dependent relationships and therapeutic approaches to them. I appreciate the efforts of Lauren Stayer for her unyielding support on all of my books and her critical feedback and help in manuscript preparation. Lorraine Penninger, my reference librarian, also was extremely helpful in identifying sources for some of the borrowed material that needed permission to reprint. Thanks to Mitchell Kearney for the back cover photograph, Bill Duane for cosmetic styling for the shoot and to Dr. Nancy Chase for her valuable support, feedback and enduring love. Finally I give special thanks to all the people not mentioned by name for their love, support and sharing of themselves in the preparation of this book.

I would like to extend my appreciation for permission to use the following credits in this book:

- Portia Nelson's poem, "Autobiography in Five Short Chapters." Copyright Portia Nelson, 1980, reprinted in The Popular Library Edition **"There's a Hole in My Sidewalk."** Copyright 1977.
- In Chapter 2 the quote by Fritjof Capra was reprinted from **The Tao of Physics,** p. xix. Copyright 1975, 1983. Reprinted by arrangement with Shambhala Publications, Inc., Boston, MA.
- In Chapter 4 "Story of the Old Farmer" by Anthony De Mello, reprinted from **Sadhana: A Way To God,** page 140, copyright 1978, Doubleday. Used with permission.
- In Chapter 8 "The Farmer and The Stranger" from **Infinity in Your Hand,** p. 14, by William H. Houff, copyright 1989, by Melior Publications. Reprinted by permission of the author.
- The 5 steps on "Pygmalion in the Classroom." From **Looking Into Classrooms** by Thomas Good and Jere Brophy. Copyright 1983, by Harper & Row, Publishers, Inc. Reprinted by permission of the publisher.
- In Chapter 12, I adapted the idea of Healograms and the related questions from the work of Arlin Peterson and Gerald Parr (1982). "Pathogram: A Visual Aid To Obtain Focus And Commitment." *Journal of Reality Therapy,* 2, 18-22.

CONTENTS

INTRODUCTION

Fasten your seat belt. You're in for the read of your life. You will find in these pages all the answers you need to get rid of your addictive thinking, to help you look within and examine who you are with a new frame of reference. It will show you how to break old addictive thought patterns and transform your life into a happy fulfilling one, no matter how painful your past. Through 10 simple principles, this book puts you in harmony with yourself and shows you how to heal your past and achieve a full and satisfying life in the present.

This book is about healing. It's about moving away from patterns of addictive thinking that prevent your life from working. It's about learning healthier and happier ways to live and establish better relationships with yourself and others. It's about now and about all the ingredients you can assemble *now* to be happy, regardless of what or why certain things happened in the past.

Five years after the death of my alcoholic father and turning 40, I still limped through life from the wounded thinking of my dysfunctional childhood. Today I have discovered in my work that the addictive thinking that we carry with us is at the root of all our unhappiness. Our addictions are not the problem; they are only symptoms of an underlying addictive way of thinking about and responding to life. We can recover and live self-satisfying lives by changing how we think about the world. True and lasting change occurs when we take the world we learned through addictive eyes and re-interpret it through healing eyes. I have turned my life around and I continue to recover from the addictive thinking I learned as a child.

This book demonstrates how you can overcome your addictive thinking. It shows you how to identify and heal addictive thought patterns. It presents 10 principles of recovery from addictive thinking. It shows how to enrich your life and achieve fulfillment by putting these principles into daily practice. It gives you simple processes and techniques for connecting with your higher self and achieving self-renewal, joy and serenity in your life.

As you begin to break the addictive thinking process that you learned in childhood and obey the healing principles, the quality of your life will improve and for the first time you will feel that you have arrived home. The 10 principles of healing can help you to:

- Untangle yourself from the web of your addictive upbringing and heal your old mental pictures.
- Create more choices for you to choose the best.
- Clear addictive thoughts and feelings from your life so that you're in a better position to receive healing and happiness.
- View your life in a more optimistic way.
- Create positive life conditions for yourself by expecting the best life has to offer.
- Establish more balance and harmony with yourself, the world and the people in it.
- Empower yourself so that you feel responsible for your life instead of victimized by it.
- Radiate positive thoughts, feelings and actions that will return to enrich your life.
- Attract people and events into your life that fit with how you think, feel and behave and mirror your healing self.
- Heal yourself from the inside out and find self-fulfillment on your inner journey.

In writing this one book, I realize that I am writing a thousand different books. Each of you who reads these pages will read the words differently because of your own preconceived ways of thinking. Each of you will filter the words through your perceptual system in your own unique way. Each of you will select and use what you need in order to profit from your individual spiritual journeys.

Bryan Robinson

CHAPTER 1

Nothing has changed but my attitude. Everything has changed.

Anthony De Mello

Are You An Addictive Thinker?

Tears streamed down my cheeks. Emotionally exhausted and slumped in my seat, all I could do when the flight attendant asked me if I wanted something to eat was wave her away with my hand. I had lost so much weight that I looked like a refugee from Dachau. During the lift-off, I didn't care if the plane crashed. Nothing mattered. I was on my way for a sunny week in Jamaica to escape the pain of breaking up from a 14-year relationship. My life was crumbling under my feet and there was nothing I could do about it. I felt like half a person. I didn't care if I lived or died. That was the spring of 1983.

I didn't know it at the time but I was living out the addictive patterns I had learned growing up in a dysfunctional family. Five years later I would discover that addictive thinking had been in my family for three generations.

My grandmother was a compulsive overeater and died from a stroke attributed to her obesity. Her son, my father, was an alcoholic who died from cirrhosis of the liver. I swore that I would never be like my "old man." I lived my first 30 years priding myself on the fact that I had "licked" the family disease because I had neither chemical nor food addictions. What I wouldn't know until midlife was that my family's addictive thinking had been passed down to me and had burrowed itself into the very core of my soul. Addictive patterns had lodged into my system from

childhood where they continued to direct my thinking,
my feelings and my behaviors. My general outlook on life
was polluted and all of my relationships eventually became
contaminated. I saw myself as a victim of a bad life and a
bad relationship.

"Why do all these horrible things keep happening to
me?" I whimpered. "Maybe a trip to the Caribbean will
ease the heartache."

All I could think about was how to get even with the
third person who came between me and my beloved. I
backpacked the hate and resentment as if they were excess
luggage weighing me down. I was so consumed with rage
that I lay awake until three or four in the morning, plot-
ting and avenging my damaged emotions. Unknowingly,
all these negative obsessions hurt no one but myself.

My addictive thinking caused me to try every avenue of
coping with my pain, except the ones that could heal me.
I clung to my resentments, saw only misery and despair,
blamed everybody else for my hardships and the breakup
of my relationship and tried geographic escape to ease my
pain. It never occurred to me that there was anything *more*
I could do about my unfortunate situation. My only op-
tion, as I saw it, was to react to life, rather than take
action. In so doing I disempowered myself by playing the
victim of a love-torn relationship. I became cynical, negative and pessimistic — all of which ricocheted, slapped
me in the face and multiplied my misery and despair.

Guaranteed Steps To Addictive Living

Everyone wants to live a happy life. But why are so
many of us miserable so much of the time, constantly
searching for inner peace with little success? Because
we're looking for it in the wrong place.

An ancient tale about Nasrudin, who lost his house key
on the way home one night, illustrates this point beautifully.

Nasrudin was down on all fours under the street lamp
searching frantically for his house key when a stranger

came by and asked him what he was looking for. Nasrudin told him he had lost the key to his house. So the stranger, being a kind man, got down on his hands and knees and helped look for it. After hours of searching with no success, the stranger asked, "Are you sure you dropped the key in this spot?" Nasrudin said, "Oh, no! I dropped it way over there in that dark alley." Frustrated and angry, the stranger lost his temper, "Then why are you looking for it here?" Nasrudin replied, "Because the light's better here under the street lamp."

Many of us are like Nasrudin. Our addictive thinking causes us to spend our lives looking in the wrong places for happiness. We keep searching in the same spot because it's familiar to us. We refuse to explore new areas that appear unfamiliar or threatening, even when they might lead to ultimate illumination. As a result, we have better success at being *unhappy* for the greater part of our lives.

Instead of following the principles that can heal our lives, we are stuck in addictive thoughts, feelings and behaviors.

Are You Stuck In Addictive Living?

If you keep repeating the following, then you, too, are stuck in addictive thinking, which inevitably leads to addicted living and eternal unhappiness:

1. *Do you beat yourself up for what you "should" have done?* Do you "should" on yourself at least two or three times a day? When you remind yourself what you "should" have done, you remind yourself that nothing you ever do is quite good enough. When you "should" on yourself, you fill yourself with shame and self-contempt and see yourself as a failure. Psychiatrist David Burns calls this "shouldy thinking." Other words like "ought" or "must" serve the same purpose. Psychologist Albert Ellis calls it "must-ur-bation."

2. *Do you put up resistance to keep things as they are?* Cling to the familiar and the routine? Won't accept anything that happens to you? Do you resist life at all costs? Try to make trees fly and stones produce milk? Try to fit your size 9 foot into a size 7 shoe? Look what happened to Cinderella's stepsisters. When these tactics don't work, do you act surprised? Then do you cry, fret and throw temper tantrums so you can stay stuck in misery and unhappiness?

3. *Do you react to life, rather than waste your time taking action when problems or worries befall you?* Do you spend all of your time reacting and getting upset and angry at problems and worries, instead of trying to solve them? Do you throw temper tantrums or blame someone else? And by all means do you always let people know how "pissed" you really are?

4. *Are you a victim?* No matter what happens to you, do you always wallow in self-pity, saying, "Poor me. Look how awful people treat me. Look how unfair life is to me. Why do people pick on me?" This will get people to feel sorry for you and maybe they will do what you want. The victim monologue is also known as the "Tammy Faye Bakker syndrome."

5. *Do you hold on to resentments?* Stay stuck in yesterday? Keep digging up the past? Hold on to old hurts or painful memories? Do you worry about the same things happening over and over again in the future, never forgiving yourself or others for the wrong they do to you? Hold it inside to get back at them? They told you that you were stupid when you were seven, so you will still feel stupid at 47.

6. *Do you want what you cannot have?* Engage in wishful thinking? Devalue what you already have and choose what you can least likely get? Then crave it and pine over it? Stop eating? Make yourself sick and throw up? Your unhappiness is guaranteed.

7. *Are you pessimistic and live by the motto that "Misery is Optimal?"* Do you continue to look at life as bleak and burdensome? Happiness may be for some peo-

ple, but it's not in the stars for you. Do you always expect the worst out of life? Think negatively, are critical of yourself and others and always look for the flaws instead of the shine? Do you dwell on how horrible life is and imagine that you'd be better off dead? Then think about how terrifying death is, too, so that there's no way out of your pessimism?

8. *Do you let fear dominate your life?* Life is serious business, and you've got to get it right. Are you terrified of people and the unexpected? Don't have fun, be silly, laugh, or enjoy life because, as Melody Beattie says, it costs money, makes noise and isn't necessary.

9. *Do you always worry about "what if" instead of "what is?"* If a loved one is late and it's raining, do you imagine the worst thing that could possibly happen and play it out over and over again in your mind? Be sure to include lots of blood, decapitation and mangled bodies. Do you think about "what if" your loved one slams into a bridge, plunges 20 feet into the water, the car explodes and his body is broken into tiny pieces and thrown in three hundred different directions? Or worry about whether or not you turned off the oven? Do you think about it catching the house ablaze, and when you pull in the driveway, your house will be in smouldering ruins? Catastrophic thinking will cause you lots of needless worry, anxiety and add crisis to your life.

10. *Do you feel unworthy?* Do you feel bad about yourself on the inside, but keep up the false front? Don't let anyone know how really undeserving you are. Make them think you're competent, even though you know and I know that you're really not. If you don't keep fooling them, they'll find out you're a fake. They'll take away your credentials, remove you from your job and ride you out of town on a rail.

11. *Are you a perpetual people pleaser?* By gaining the approval of others, you will feel better about yourself. There once was a man named Sam who would do anything to please others. He was so encumbered

with low self-image that he lay face up in the middle of a busy street saying he had taken a job as a speed bump. Make yourself a speed bump if you have to, but above all make sure others approve of what you say and do. If you're real industrious, you can open your own business called "Speed Bumps R Us."

12. *Do you neglect yourself?* You'll feel better by forgetting about yourself and losing yourself in the needs of others. Eat lots of junk food, stay busy and burn yourself out. By ignoring your own emotional and health needs and caring for others, your worries will vanish. And so will you!

13. *Do you look for things outside yourself to make you happy?* Do you have plenty of unsafe sex, take drugs, overeat, gamble, work compulsively, stay drunk or overspend? These things will keep your mind off your problems until happiness falls in your lap. As a child, keeping busy with schoolwork was the beginning of my addiction because it kept my mind off the trouble at home. At school I was the kind of kid who, as we were being dismissed for Christmas vacation, would raise my hand and say, "Mrs. Higginbottom, you forgot to assign homework over Christmas vacation." I was a big hit with my classmates.

14. *If all else fails, do you move to a new apartment, town, country or continent?* Are most people unhappy because of where they live or work? The grass is always greener on the other side. You'll be happier on the beaches of Maui, in the Amazon Jungle, in San Francisco or New York City. Anywhere is better than where you are.

Core Beliefs of Addictive Thinkers

There is a grain of truth to each of these exaggerations. How many of us have spent our entire lives unconsciously following these steps to addictive living? It's no wonder our lives are not working. Practicing these steps made me enormously successful at being unhappy. I learned at an early age that life is burdensome, full of worry and misery, and happiness was not to be mine. No one ever told me directly. But that was the message I received growing up in a dysfunctional home. Life was defined for me as chaotic, full of stress and crisis — an uphill battle.

As a small child I learned to fight to survive. I learned that I had to take control of situations or they would consume and ultimately destroy me. I learned to resist, to try to control, to be a victim, to have a gloomy outlook, to be ruled by fear, to always expect the worst in every situation, to torture myself by worrying about things that would never happen, to feel unworthy, to please others, to neglect myself and to look outside myself for happiness. I used to hear people say, "Happiness is a state of mind" or that "Misery is optional" and I would laugh hysterically at the thought that I could have any say-so over my own personal destiny. After all, look what a terrible childhood I had!

Due to my addictive thinking, I had a faulty belief system. The major core beliefs that addictive thinkers share are:

- *Self-Flawed Thinking.* Something must be wrong with me. I am inadequate, unworthy and unlovable.
- *Helpless Thinking.* There is nothing I can do to change my life.
- *Pessimistic Thinking.* Life is chaotic and stressful and full of misery and despair.
- *Catastrophic Thinking.* Something terrible will probably happen, so I must stay prepared by always expecting the worst.
- *Resistance Thinking.* Life is an uphill battle and I must fight to enforce my way, resist what I don't want and cling to keep things as they are.
- *Self-Victimized Thinking.* Other people and other situations are to blame for my hardships.
- *Telescopic Thinking.* I always feel like a failure because I ignore my successes and focus on my downfalls.

- *Blurred Boundary Thinking.* I need another person to make me a whole person or if I let others get to know me, they might not like me.
- *Resentful Thinking.* I will never forgive them for what they did to me.
- *All-or-None Thinking.* I'm either the best or the worst; there is no in-between.
- *Perfectionistic Thinking.* Things have to be perfect for me to be happy and nothing I ever do is good enough.
- *People-Pleasing Thinking.* If I can get others to like me, I'll feel better about myself.
- *Wishful Thinking.* I wish I could have the things I cannot have because the things I have are of no value.
- *Serious Thinking.* Playing and having fun is a waste of time because life is too full of problems.
- *Externalized Thinking.* Happiness can be found in the external world so changing the outer circumstances of my life will fix how I feel inside.

This book is based on the premise that *our thoughts create our physical and emotional realities.* The ways in which we think actually are manifested in the material world.

Everything that happens is a thought before it is an action.

As an example, think of something simple that you can draw in less than a minute, such as a stick figure or a flower (your merit as an artist doesn't count). Now draw it in the margin of this page. You just transformed your thought into a physical reality.

The movie, *Gone With The Wind,* The Washington Memorial, Beethoven's Fifth, the houses on your street, your car, your television, the seat you're sitting in, this book you're reading now — all began in the human mind as a thought. How you plan to confront a hostile friend, ask your boss for a raise or resolve conflict in your love relationship are thoughts before they are actions.

In the same way we create our physical world, we can create just about anything we want by how we think. All of us have images of events and interactions before they occur on the physical plane. Everything we create, from making a cake to our addictions, starts in the human mind by our patterns of thinking. Our addictive thinking patterns cause us to create chaotic and addictive lifestyles. To change our unhappy lives, we must first change our addictive ways of thinking.

As Anthony De Mello said, *"Nothing has changed but my attitude. Everything has changed."* Healthy thinking creates the manifestation of healthy and happy lives in the physical world.

Just as water takes the form of the vessel it fills, our thoughts mold the character of our lives. We create our life conditions through our thinking. Whether the addiction is to alcohol and drugs, co-dependent relationships, food, work, sex, gambling or spending money, the addictive-thinking patterns are the same. Living by these core beliefs blocks recovery and keeps us stuck in addictive thinking and living. The reason we see one addiction substituted for another is because the belief system has not changed. Addictions are passed from one generation to the next because parents unknowingly pass their addictive perceptions of the world to their children.

Although children may switch their addictions, their addictive thinking remains the same. Recovery is a simple matter of identifying our addictive-thinking patterns and changing them to healthier ways of perceiving the world. Healthy feelings and behaviors automatically follow healthy thoughts.

A Self-Test For Addictive Thinking

Many of us are searching frantically for happiness and fulfillment. But we are looking in the wrong place. Wayne Dyer, in his book, *You'll Believe It When You See It*, puts it this way:

> "We live inside, we think inside, our humanity resides within, yet we spend time ceaselessly looking outside of ourselves for the answers because we fail to illuminate the inside with our thoughts. We resist the principle that thought is everything we are because it seems easier to look outside."

Once Nasrudin looks in the alley, he will illuminate his life and find his house key. Once we begin to look within ourselves, we will illuminate our thoughts and find the answers for breaking our addictive-thinking patterns.

Are you an addictive thinker? If so, chances are that you are contaminating your own life and that of friends, business associates and loved ones. If you are a parent, you could be passing your addictive thinking on to your children.

Here is a self-test to help you find out. Read each of the 25 statements in the box and decide how much each one pertains to you. After you have answered all 25 statements, add up the numbers in the blanks for your total score.

A score of 25 to 54 = You are not an addictive thinker.
A score of 55 to 69 = You are a mildly addictive thinker.
A score of 70 to 100 = You are a highly addictive thinker.

Are You An Addictive Thinker?

1 point   =   never true
2 points =   seldom true
3 points =   often true
4 points =   always true

Put the number that best fits you in the blank beside each statement.

_____ 1. I am afraid to let other people get close to me.

_____ 2. I fear the unexpected.

_____ 3. I look for the flaws instead of the shine in most situations.

_____ 4. I feel unworthy of other people's love.

_____ 5. I feel inferior to other people.

_____ 6. I have a compulsive habit, such as over-working, overeating, gambling, compulsive shopping or alcohol or drug addiction.

_____ 7. I neglect my own needs in favor of caring for the needs of others.

_____ 8. I have a lot of buried feelings from the past, such as anger, fear, shame or sadness.

_____ 9. I seek approval and affirmation from others through people-pleasing, perfectionism or compulsive overachievement.

_____ 10. I take myself too seriously and find it hard to be playful and have fun.

_____ 11. I have developed health or physical problems from excessive worry, stress or burnout.

_____ 12. I have an overpowering need to control.

(continued)

_____ 13. I have difficulty expressing my true feelings.

_____ 14. I dislike myself.

_____ 15. My life seems to be in crisis.

_____ 16. I think that I am a victim of life.

_____ 17. I am afraid of being abandoned by those I love.

_____ 18. I criticize myself or put myself down.

_____ 19. I expect the worst out of most situations.

_____ 20. When I make a mistake, I feel that *I* am the mistake.

_____ 21. I blame others for the troubles that befall me.

_____ 22. I live in the past.

_____ 23. I am closed to new ideas or different ways of doing things.

_____ 24. I spend a lot of time being upset or angry about things that happen to me.

_____ 25. I feel lonely and isolated even when surrounded by people.

_____ TOTAL SCORE

CHAPTER 2

The real voyage consists not in seeking new landscapes but in having new eyes.

Marcel Proust

The 10 Principles Of Healing

None of us with sound mind would leap off a ledge into the Grand Canyon because we know that if we defy the law of gravity, we would fall down and not up. Yet we leap off the cliff of our personal lives everyday with our addictive thinking.

In the same ways, addictive thinking defies the Principles of Healing and prevents our lives from working. The 10 Principles of Healing teach us to build a strong fence around the cliff, but addictive thinking tells us to put an ambulance in the valley below.

We keep getting involved in unhealthy relationships that hurt us. We go back to the same people for the same rejections. We keep trying to solve problems in the same old ways that we already know don't work. We resist change and cling to sameness. We live in the past. We want most in life what we cannot have. And we neglect and condemn ourselves daily. The list goes on and on.

What Are The Principles Of Healing?

Our thoughts, feelings and behaviors no longer have to be governed by our addictive upbringing. We can unleash ourselves from this legacy, but we *must* believe that it is possible. We also must be willing to give up addictive thought patterns and pursue and persist in healthier ways of thinking.

We do this by learning the *10 Principles Of Healing* and bringing our lives into alignment with them. These principles or laws operate all around us even now as you read this book, just like physical laws such as the law of gravity.

In his book, *The Tao of Physics*, physicist Fritjof Capra shows how the Eastern spiritual disciplines and modern physics hold the same world view:

> I was sitting by the ocean one late summer afternoon, watching the waves rolling in and feeling the rhythm of my breathing, when I suddenly became aware of my whole environment as being engaged in a gigantic cosmic dance. Being a physicist, I knew that the sand, rocks, water and air around me were made of vibrating molecules and atoms, and that these consisted of particles which interacted with one another by creating and destroying other particles. I knew also that the earth's atmosphere was continually bombarded by showers of "cosmic rays," particles of high energy undergoing multiple collisions as they penetrated the air. All this was familiar to me from my research in high-energy physics, but until that moment I had only experienced it through graphs, diagrams and mathematical theories. As I sat on that beach my former experiences came to life; I *saw* cascades of energy coming down from outer space, in which particles were created and destroyed in rhythmic pulses; I *saw* the atoms of the elements and those of my body participating in this cosmic dance of energy; I felt its rhythm and I *heard* its sound and at that moment I *knew* that this was the Dance of Shiva, the Lord of Dancers worshipped by the Hindus. (p. xix).

In much the same way, the 10 Principles of Healing, although ordinarily unseen and unmeasured, parallel the physical laws. The Principles of Healing integrate the spiritual aspects of recovery so that we can see and use the consequences of our own actions for personal growth and fulfillment.

If someone holding an apple lets it go, you would predict that it would fall to the ground. Your prediction is based partly on your past experience and on the gravitational pull of the earth. Sir Isaac Newton discovered the law of gravity as he sat under an apple tree. When an apple dropped to the ground near him, he wanted to know why the apple fell *down* and not *up*. From this simple incident

Newton developed the law of gravity to explain the behavior of the earth, planets, moon, sun, stars and aster-
oids. No one would defy the law of gravity or they would
be headed for trouble.

We avoid touching the metal handles of hot cooking
pots unless we use a potholder because we know that
metal conducts heat. We refrain from touching an exposed
wire while standing in the bathtub, because we know
the end result could be lethal: the law is that *water conducts electricity*. Because we know these principles to be
true, we obey them.

There are similar principles that govern our thoughts,
feelings and actions and thus govern the nature of our
relationships and the quality of our lives. Because these
principles are not as precise as the laws of physics, we
keep making the same mistakes over and over. And we
continue to get involved in the same co-dependent relationships that end in disillusionment and unhappiness.

In other words we continue to follow our addictive thinking and to defy the Principles of Healing. In recovery we
learn the difference between addictive thoughts and healing thoughts, and we change our behaviors to fit the healing principles.

As I began to change, my new thinking had a positive
effect on my feelings and behaviors, which, in turn,
changed how others responded to me. By renouncing my
addictive thinking and abiding by the Principles of Healing,
my life began to work with more ease. The 10 Principles
of Healing are a blend of many viewpoints, some ancient
and some new. They are based on the notion that our
thoughts create our physical reality and our experiences
of life. We are what we think we are and we can change
ourselves by changing our thinking.

*By changing how we think, we can literally change how our
personal lives are manifested.*

We can actually transform hardships, unhappiness and
despair into a life of ease, happiness and serenity simply
by changing our addictive patterns of thinking into healing
patterns of thinking. These principles are as follows:

The 10 Principles Of Healing

1. *Principle of Perception.* Our perceptions of ourselves and the world are shaped by mental pictures of past reality that can be changed.

2. *Principle of Choice.* We always have the power to choose how we will think, feel and behave, no matter how hopeless our lives seem to be.

3. *Principle of Vacuum.* Getting rid of addictive thoughts and feelings clears a space for us to receive healing and happiness in our lives.

4. *Principle of Optimism.* We can create a positive and happy life by taking an optimistic outlook and by looking on the positive side of situations rather than the negative side.

5. *Principle of Expectation.* Our expectations have self-fulfilling effects that create our experiences and thus our experiences of life become whatever we expect them to be.

6. *Principle of Harmony.* Our lives work when we align our thoughts, feelings and actions to fit into the grand harmony of nature, rather than resist the natural forces of the universe.

7. *Principle of Empowerment.* We are empowered when we think of ourselves as survivors instead of victims of life and when we accept responsibility for our thoughts, feelings and actions.

8. *Principle of the Boomerang.* The thoughts we put out from within eventually come back to us in one form or another, just like a boomerang.

9. *Principle of Magnetism.* We attract people into our lives who think, feel and behave like us and thus people closest to us are mirrors of ourselves.

10. *Principle of the Inner Guru.* Healing addictive thoughts and lifestyles comes from the inside out, not the outside in.

Understanding these principles and how they are en-
forced and following them like we do the physical laws can
change and enrich our lives.

All of us are criminals. Not because we've broken the
legal system, but because we've broken the healing laws.
When we break these principles, we pay. We sentence
ourselves to self-abuse through misery and addiction.
Breaking these laws keeps our lives from working and
leads to emotional imprisonment. No one will arrest us
but ourselves and the penalty for breaking these laws is a
life sentence of addictive living. We can stop breaking laws
once we know what they are. And when we do break
them, we can parole ourselves through self-forgiveness.

Those of us on a spiritual journey are shedding addictive thought patterns and transforming our old ways into
new and healing ways of thinking, feeling, and behaving.
We are on a never-ending path that continually helps us
improve the quality of our lives on a daily basis. We do
this by following the 10 Principles of Healing, that once
learned, bring us serenity and happiness.

Applying The Principles Of Healing

No matter how dysfunctional your family was, you no
longer have to live in the shadows of parental addictive
thinking. Our misery and unhappiness are not determined by past and present circumstances. They are determined by our addictive thoughts about those circumstances and how we respond to these mental mindsets.
All of us carry pictures of reality in our minds based on
perceptions we develop from our upbringing. These pictures or mindsets develop from our own unique family
and cultural experiences. *These perceptions are not reality; they
are our interpretations of reality as it is filtered through our eyes.*

In our society, for example, we have many words to
describe colors — pink, orange, yellow, teal and so on. But
many societies have far fewer words and as a result, they
see fewer colors than we do. Eskimos have many words to

describe snow, while the English language has only a few. So the Eskimo thinks about and sees more kinds of snow than English-speaking people because he develops more mental pictures of snow.

In much the same way we develop addictive perceptions of ourselves and the world living in dysfunctional families. These dysfunctional mindsets contaminate our feelings and actions which cause others to react to us in dysfunctional ways. So through dysfunctional eyes, we create a cycle of interaction that is self-reinforcing because it develops into dysfunctional relationships and addictive lifestyles. The Principles of Healing help us break this cycle. They help us see that it is not what other people do that upsets us; it is the patterns of addictive thoughts that we carry in our heads that upset us. Our lives are governed by our addictive mindsets that have shaped our thoughts and decided how we must "react" to daily occurrences. Change our addictive mindsets and we eliminate the unhappiness.

Once we understand that it is our addictive thoughts and perceptions that prevent our lives from working, and not the reality of the world, we stop reacting and start acting.

In a nutshell our unhappiness does not come from *outside* reality; it comes from our *inner* interpretation of reality that we make through our mental pictures of the past. As long as things work out to suit us (match our mental mindsets), we are happy. But when something happens or someone does something that goes against our wishes or doesn't live up to our expectations (doesn't fit our inner pictures of reality), we become unhappy. This addictive thinking puts us at the mercy of other people and events to determine the quality with which we live our lives. Living this way, we will be miserable most of the time.

The fact that what upsets one person may not upset another person demonstrates that anger or hurt do not come from objective reality but from each individual's interpretation of it.

For example, the same event that upsets Sally, who is in a co-dependent relationship, does not upset Mildred, who is not in a co-dependent relationship. Sally gets upset when her husband goes bowling without her because, she says, "He'd rather be with his friends than me." Mildred enjoys the time apart and believes it is healthy for the relationship. The outside facts are the same for both marriages: Both husbands bowl together on Thursdays and love their wives equally the same. But the two wives have two different perceptions of the same reality. Clearly the objective reality of bowling is not the source of upset; Sally's perception is the cause of her upset. She blames the outside event of her husband's bowling for her insecurities when, in fact, they come from her addictive thoughts and perceptions that she developed in childhood. Her thoughts cause her to have feelings of rejection which lead to angry outbursts toward her husband. He, in turn, feels frustrated and angry because of her jealousy toward his bowling companion

Many of us, like Sally, often blame our discontent on someone else, some situation or our dysfunctional past: overly strict parents, an abusive lover, ill health or a traumatic accident. The list is endless. But yesterday is gone forever. All we have left is today's mental scrapbook of past events. We cannot change those events, but we can change how we look at the old pictures when we open the scrapbook. We can even clean out the scrapbook to make room for different pictures of today.

The Principles of Healing help you change your outlook on life. You begin to see past and present events as opportunities for growth and improvement. Instead of bemoaning what life deals, you accept it and go on, making the best of what you have today. When you are unhappy or things are not going right, you can change your addictive thinking. Old patterns of thinking will not automatically shift by themselves, but you can correct them with the Principles of Healing.

Sally began to realize, through the Principles of Healing, that her interpretation of the situation contributed to her feelings of rejection. Taking a healthier outlook and employing these principles in her life caused Sally's feelings and behaviors to change. Sally's changed behaviors caused her husband to respond to her in a more positive way. Sally resolved the dilemma by changing *her* behavior instead of expecting her husband to change his.

The Principles of Healing take you through a series of stages that help you make changes in yourself that result in changes in the quality of your life from top to bottom.

1. You understand that your perceptions are addictive and how they become that way.
2. You realize that your addictive thinking is keeping you stuck in an unhappy way of living.
3. You abandon your old thought pattern and make way for new and healthier thinking.
4. You put the 10 Principles of Healing into practice through conscious effort.
5. You replace addictive thinking with healing thinking through an ongoing commitment to continued inner growth and change.

You can apply the 10 Principle of Healing to any part of your life: to fears, relationships, jobs or your addictions. These principles have their own self-reinforcing effect. As you practice them and see them work, you become more confident that you can change your life. This confidence strengthens your faith in this new way of thinking and eventually it becomes a part of you.

Through Healing Eyes

There once was a starfish who lived in the ocean. "Pardon me," he said to the whale. "Could you tell me where I can find the sea?"

"You are already in the sea," replied the whale. "It is all around you."

"This?" replied the starfish. "This is just the ocean. I'm looking for the sea."

The frustrated starfish swam away to continue searching for the sea.

"Look no further," yelled the wise old whale after him, "*Seaing* is a matter of *seeing!*"

As you make the healing shift in how you see your life, you remain the same person on the outside. You may keep the same job and the same relationships. You may still get angry and impatient sometimes and there will be occasions when you will feel sad or disappointed. Your transformation happens on the inside. You look at your life in a different way. You see things with new insight and greater clarity.

Teilhard de Chardin described this change as "ever more perfect eyes in a world in which there is always more to see." You don't swim around the answers like the starfish, looking and wishing for something that is already his. Instead, you see what is already yours and are grateful for it. You have made the shift from looking at your life through addictive eyes to seeing your life through healing eyes.

By Breaking Your Addictive Thinking Patterns, You Can Move From . . .

Addictive Living	To Self-Esteem
Addictive perceptions	Healing perceptions
Reacting	Acting
Pessimism	Optimism
Helplessness	Empowerment
Inability to create life experiences	Ability to create life experiences
Sending and receiving negative thoughts	Sending and receiving positive thoughts
Attracting the negative	Attracting the positive
Holding on to resentments	Letting go of resentments
Pleasing others	Self-acceptance
Resistance	Harmony
Self-shame	Self-love

When we are spiritually enlightened, nothing changes except the way we perceive, the way we use our minds.

William H. Houff

The Principle
Of Perception

Our perceptions of ourselves and the world are shaped by mental pictures of past reality that can be changed.

Perception is the window to our minds. It governs our reality and determines the quality of our lives. Our perceptions — good or bad — are formed early in life and depend upon the cultural norms and daily experiences under which we grow up. As children, we are like clay because we are still under mental construction. As we grow from childhood, the words we hear and the attitudes, feelings and actions that parents exhibit mold our perceptions of the everyday world. The perceptions we are exposed to in childhood influence the mental outlooks we manifest in our adult interactions. Perceptual restrictions in childhood can have lasting effects that shape adult lives.

Perceptual studies conducted with animals have human implications. In a laboratory experiment at Cambridge University in England the vision of baby kittens was restricted to horizontal lines from birth. They were never exposed to vertical lines while growing up. Once grown, the adult cats could recognize horizontal lines (——) but not vertical ones (|). They could jump on table tops, but they consistently bumped into the vertical table legs. Vertical lines were not part of the adult cat's perceptual reality because they never experienced them as kittens. You might even say that because of their restricted past, the cats had a restricted view of reality.

The same is true for those of us from families that think addictively. The ways in which we are taught to perceive the world determine our mental outlook. We essentially have our perceptions restricted as a result of living in addictive-thinking homes. Early experiences in our families of origin set our sights in a certain direction and we begin to perceive the world as it is shown to us through the eyes of our parents. When we live in dysfunctional families, our perceptions become addictive, and we carry addictive outlooks with us even as adults. Our addictive past experiences determine what we see in the world around us.

Something Must Be Wrong With Me

Growing up in dysfunction, we learn a host of distorted beliefs about ourselves and others which interfere with our ability to feel and behave in self-enhancing ways. Double messages confuse children and put them in a double bind. They are confused by what they are told and what they see.

Deidre, now 21, expressed her childhood confusion over this double bind:

My mother was always drunk, and she beat me from the time I was four. While she hit me, she'd say: "You're a good little girl." She was on the couch and sandwiched me between her feet and the coffee table pushing me hard against it with her feet. The whole time she told me one thing and did another. I remember thinking, "Well why are you hurting me if I'm a good girl?"

These conflicting messages distort our perceptions of "normal" and appropriate. Carried into adulthood, they can paralyze us in social situations and intimate relationships because we are unsure of ourselves.

Little Molly was a bouncy nine-year-old who swelled with delight when her mother beckoned to her with open arms. "Come here, sweetheart, and give me a kiss. Mommie loves you so much!" Expecting to be comforted in the security and warmth of her mother's arms, Molly was met instead with a sharp slap across her face and a belligerent reprimand, "You are a bad little girl!" Molly didn't know that her mother was schizophrenic; all little Molly knew was that she was a bad little girl, a perception that she still carries at age 46.

Parental inconsistency and unpredictability are hallmarks of addictive families. I was perplexed by my own father's personality changes and wondered how he could always act like nothing out of the ordinary had happened the morning after drunken skirmishes. While my family still carried around anger from the previous night, my father had transformed into a sweet, gentle and caring man. It was a kind and considerate father who dropped us off at the seven o'clock movie and promised through genuine smiles to be back by nine. But it was a snarling monster who returned at 12 o'clock or never returned at all. I didn't realize at the time that his blackouts prevented him from remembering the events of the night before. I thought something was wrong with my view.

Children from addictive-thinking households often walk on eggshells, desperately trying to second-guess parental expectations. The consistency and orderliness of the outside world are absent at home. Rules, when they do exist, are switched around daily so that children never know what to expect. Many of these children have witnessed their parents out of control or violent in some way. They themselves have been slapped, hit or thrown around. The see-saw upbringing under the addictive parent arouses anxiety. Children do everything in their power to change, so that their lives will become stable, predictable and manageable.

The lesson I learned from these experiences was that "something must be wrong with me." It was not the addictive situation in which I was living that was wrong. I was "wrong." Children have difficulty separating themselves from the addictive thinking. Instead, we develop

addictive thoughts and internalize the shame, embar-
rassment and other experienced emotions as part of who
we are. So when we make mistakes, we think and feel
that *we* are the mistakes.

Sometimes the addictive thoughts of "something must
be wrong with me" are passed down to children through
the opposite extreme: Not from chaos or inconsistency,
but from parental perfectionism that is impossible to meet.

In the case of 42-year-old Irene, both her parents had
been raised in alcoholic homes. They were determined to
give Irene and her brother a better upbringing than they
had as children. Alcohol was never around as Irene grew
up, but her mother became a placater and her father a
workaholic. Irene's father was such a high achiever that
he got his Thank-You notes out the day after Christmas.
He set high standards both for himself and his children.
There were lots of "shoulds" in Irene's family. Her father,
a traveling salesman, was on the road most weekdays, so
she saw him only on weekends. He gave her a dollar every
time she read *How To Win Friends And Influence People*. Says
Irene, "That book emphasizes the people-pleasing stuff —
tuning in to others, making them feel important. Underneath all that gentle manipulation is the basic need to
control how others feel about me."

Irene remembers that there was a sense of something
missing as a child. She always wished there was more
closeness in her family. She always thought it was her
fault that she was unhappy and lacking as a child:

> "My dad was a good provider, a regular church-going man.
> My parents worked hard to provide for us and to send us to
> summer camp. They wanted to be *Ozzie and Harriet*, and they
> tried real hard to be. But I never felt loved and accepted, even
> though I know my parents meant well. So with such a perfect
> upbringing, there had to be something wrong with me for want-
> ing to have intimate feeling conversations and relationships and
> for feeling like I wasn't loved or accepted.

Irene became deeply enmeshed in addictive thinking.
For most of her adult life, she obeyed all the laws of

addictive thinking by bypassing conflict, neglecting her own needs and being overly accommodating to other people. Being accepted and understood became her major coping devices — being a good girl and a good daughter and doing all the things she was supposed to do. She was always willing to forfeit her own wants and needs by yielding to the whims of others. As a compulsive overeater, she stuffed herself with food to fill that same void that her father had tried to fill all his life with work.

Irene's parents obviously had her best interests at heart. We all want the best for our children. But unless parents learn to break the addictive thinking patterns under which they grew up, their perception of "the best" for their kids is restricted, defined and distorted by the same addictive thinking that their parents passed on to them.

Many of us from these homes adopt our parents' addictive perceptions as our own — even when they don't match what we see. And we live with an unspeakable deep feeling that "something is wrong with us." We learn to look at the dark side of life, rather than the bright. The lens is distorted so that we think only the worst can happen.

Perceptual Illusions

One of the universal truths is that the world as we have perceived it is not the way the world is at all. The Principle of Perception says that our reality is not reality but a perception or picture of reality that we created in our heads. Psychologist Kurt Lewin's field theory holds that if you believe you are unworthy, unlikeable or ugly — even though others do not perceive you that way — your impression that "I am an undeserving person" is still a fact within your life space. This misconception or illusion influences your behavior as much as if it were objectively true. Field theory says that we do not behave on the basis of objective reality but on the basis of what we perceive to be true, whether our impressions match objective reality or are illusions.

Many of the feelings we have about ourselves and others are simply illusions. A good example of this occurred while I was waiting for a bus near a busy intersection in Honolulu. A traffic cop was talking to a woman who was stopped in the middle of the street. Traffic was tied up and horns were blowing. A woman standing behind me complained loudly and obnoxiously about her disdain for law enforcement officers.

"If he wants to give her a ticket, why doesn't he pull her over to the side. That's what makes me sick about cops! They have to throw their weight around. He's got traffic tied up for miles!" The woman continued to blast the officer as she walked off in the distance waving her arms in protest, carrying her misperceptions of that event with her forever.

The police officer raised the hood of the car, sat in the driver's seat and tried to start the engine with no success. My perception was that the car had stalled in traffic and the officer was merely trying to help. Obviously this woman's anger was dominated by her perception of past experiences with policemen. Shortly, I saw the driver of the car go into a telephone booth while the policeman lay across the front seat looking under the dashboard.

As my bus pulled up and I got on board, I heard one of the passengers say, "Look! Someone abandoned their car in the middle of the street! What's this world coming to?" A third perception of the same event occurred as the passenger, new on the scene, filtered the experience through his own past personal experiences.

A common complaint from adult children of alcoholics is that the sober parent would pretend that nothing was wrong even when the house was being torn apart. In their well-meaning attempts to smooth over family problems, nonalcoholic parents often pretend everything is okay and insist that the children perceive things that way too. They accomplish this by invalidating the child's reality: "Your father isn't an alcoholic. He's just depressed right now. He'll get over it."

The "elephant-in-the-living-room" syndrome occurs when children are led to believe that they are seeing a perceptual illusion.

Let's suppose, for instance, that Dad gets drunk, falls and hits his head on the coffee table. The mother and daughter come into their living room and see him spread-eagled on the floor with blood oozing from his forehead. Mother doesn't react or say anything. Denying that things are as bad as they are or pretending they never happened causes children to become confused and have difficulty trusting their own perceptions. They begin to repress their suspicions and minimize their feelings. They begin to believe that the traumatic things that horrified them are not all that bad. They learn to numb their feelings. Eventually children from dysfunctional families will deny their own perceptions and those of outsiders who try to convince them that the family has a problem.

After years of having perceptual illusions, we think that our perceptions are wrong and that we cannot trust our own view of things. Experts tell us that since we see what we expect to see, we view the world through biased eyes and seldom see things as they actually are.

Changing Our Lenses Of The Past

We never see objects, events, people or even ourselves in isolation. Instead, we interpret everything based on the context it's in. As children we interpret our lives as good, bad, pleasant, chaotic or whatever — against the background of events that take place in our lives. The feelings we have about ourselves — confident, attractive, ugly, shameful — also depend upon the background we grew up in. When we feel shame, unloved, guilt, self-contempt, we have merely internalized the addictive thinking of the background we grew up in. When we feel confident, loved, happy, valued, we have internalized the tone of our backgrounds.

This is how our perceptions become distorted at an early age and we become addictive thinkers. As adults we perceive ourselves as unworthy and shameful. Life is perceived as painful, frustrating, full of misery and despair. We cannot separate ourselves from the addictive way of looking at life. We have trouble separating our identities from our behaviors. If we do something wrong, shame and guilt surface as we confuse the action with ourselves and jam them all together in our minds. We feel that we are bad human beings. So we look through addictive eyes and see only the dark side of life. We pass the addictive thinking on to friends, spouses and lovers, and tragically to our own children.

These mental pictures can be changed. Just as our perceptions are biased toward one angle — negative thinking and pessimism — we have the power to change these addictive views by finding the other side of life that our minds overlook. Healing comes as we begin to look more objectively at our lives, change our perceptions and reinterpret our past and present from a healthier standpoint. Spiritual enlightenment is simply changing the way we perceive the world. As we change the way we use our minds and the old unhealthy pictures in our heads, we begin to heal ourselves. By changing our perceptions, we can overcome fears and worries and shed limitations that hold us back from growing into full human beings.

We may have been taught that we are nothing without another person and that we cannot be happy without an intimate relationship. This is an illusion that when dropped, allows us to be happy without the need for another person to make us complete. Clinging to incorrect self-labels is a common self-defeating habit of addictive thinkers. We can unload those old erroneous lenses of the past. As we learn to view ourselves through healthier lenses, we realize we are okay just as we are.

Once we begin to separate ourselves from addictive thinking, we see that we are not the problem, but are separate from it.

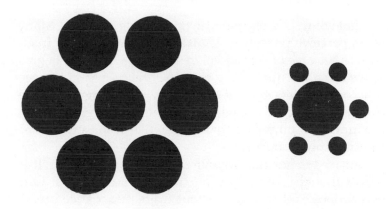

Figure 3.1. Which of the center dots is larger?

Look at the dots in the figure. Which one of the middle dots is bigger? The one surrounded by a circle of large dots? Or the one surrounded by a circle of tiny dots? The answer is they're both the same. This is a perceptual illusion. It's the surrounding dots that fool us into thinking one is larger than the other.

Let's suppose you are the dot in the center. Let's say the large dots stand for an extremely addictive-thinking family. The small dots represent a non-addictive thinking family. Although you look smaller surrounded by the addictive family and you look larger surrounded by the nonaddictive family, you're the exact same person in either case. You can see this when you look at the center dots in isolation. Once we learn to look objectively at our early lives, we begin to separate ourselves from the confusion and pain that we're still carrying with us. We realize that we are *not* the craziness and we are *not* the problems, although we have, in many instances, become them. We also learn to trust our perceptions and not let the addictive surroundings cloud our thinking.

Untangling

Untangling is a big part of the healing process. Many of us perceive ourselves as distorted, imperfect or inadequate because of our addictive thoughts. Healing begins as we learn the untangling process. Once we begin to see that our perceptions of ourselves and the world are clouded by our addictive upbringing, we learn that we can untangle ourselves from addictive mindsets to see the truth about ourselves.

Our past is not real anymore. It is only an illusion. It is only a thought carried by our memories of events. Our perceptions and thoughts about a life experience create our emotions and our reactions, not the life experience itself. It's as if we took a photograph of the past and carried it in our brain. The photograph itself is not the past. It is only our interpretation of the past, an interpretation that was filtered through our addictive thought processes, an interpretation that can be changed. So when we live in the past, we experience our memories of the event, not the actual event.

Everyone has a different reality of the same experience. There are many different ways to look at the past. Our memories of the past are ours exclusively and often do not match those of others who had the same experience. We can change our thoughts that were developed through addictive eyes. We can take a second look through healing eyes and make a healthier photograph of our past and reinterpret the memories by looking at our experiences from a different angle. Making this perceptual change in my own life was the beginning of my healing transformation.

The following simple exercise illustrates that point. Look at the square superimposed over the concentric circles. The sides look wobbly and misshapen. This is a perceptual illusion caused by the background. Let's suppose you are the misshapen square, and the concentric circles in the backdrop represent your addictive family background. When you remove the square from its background, you see that it is perfectly square and not wobbly at all.

Untangling helps you see the truth about yourself: that your negative and unhealthy self-image is simply an illusion — a distortion of reality caused by living in an addictive-thinking environment. In order to see ourselves as we truly are (healthy), we must take ourselves out of the addictive background that distorts our view of ourselves. We make new and healthier interpretations based on recovery. We see that we are okay and that the relationships that we were enmeshed in contributed to our addictive thinking. Those of us currently living in co-dependent relationships can use this technique to mentally separate ourselves from the dysfunction and to establish healthy boundaries.

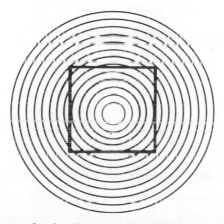

Figure 3.2. The background in this figure distorts the square, just as addictive family backgrounds can distort our self-images.

In our daily affairs this technique can help us to separate our mistakes and wrongdoings from who we are. We don't have to become the mistake. When we make a mistake, we can admit our downfalls without the addictive feelings of shame and guilt. We are human, and human beings make mistakes. Loving ourselves unconditionally, no matter what our shortcomings, and forgiving ourselves for making mistakes allow us to conquer unhealthy feelings and to untangle our tangled lives.

Self-Parenting

Joe, who came from a dysfunctional family, spent half his adult life complaining that he never had two "real" parents who could give him the kind of love and care his friends had. As early as Joe could remember, his father awakened him with, "Get your lazy ass out of bed!" and jerked the covers off his son's bed. Until he was 38, Joe perceived himself as shiftless and unproductive, even though he was a compulsive workaholic determined to prove his father wrong. In recovery Joe learned that he had developed a mental picture of himself as reflected through his father's addictive eyes. Self-parenting helped Joe see himself through healing eyes as the worthy, competent and lovable person that he really is.

Self-parenting helps us do the healing for ourselves that we never got from loving and nurturing parents in childhood. Now that we are grown, we can change our perceptions by taking responsibility for ourselves. We can give ourselves the love and caring we may have missed as children. We can nurture ourselves, be good to ourselves and expect the best that life has to offer.

How we start the morning sets the tone for the whole day. How we start our days in childhood sets the tone for the rest of our lives. When you were a child, how did your parents awaken you in the mornings? What did they say? What did they do? Try to recall what mornings were like. Maybe they didn't awaken you and you felt abandoned or uncared for. Perhaps they were hostile like Joe's father and you felt angry or hurt.

Self-Parenting Exercise

Think about what you would have liked your parents to say and do; then say and do those things for yourself now. Perhaps they were loving and gentle and there's nothing you'd change about your mornings. If so, awaken yourself with that same loving and gentleness that you got when you were young. Close your eyes and create it in your mind. See the situation and hear the words. What feelings come up? Talk about them with someone close to you, or write them in the space below.

CHAPTER 4

Man does not simply exist, but always decides what his existence will be, what he will become in the next moment.

Viktor Frankl

The Principle Of Choice

We always have the power to choose how we will think, feel and behave no matter how hopeless our lives seem to be.

During his three grim years of confinement at Auschwitz and other Nazi camps, Viktor Frankl lived through brutal treatment. He was separated from his family, deprived of food, stripped naked to be subjected to the harsh elements and robbed of all human dignity and respect. Still, through all the suffering and degradation, he always saw choices for himself and made them each day. Starving and freezing to death, he chose to relive in his mind a more pleasant moment with his loving wife or to recreate the memory of a warm spring day in a meadow. He sought meaning in his personal tragedy, and his power of choice helped him survive the holocaust, giving him renewed satisfaction and purpose in life.

Frankl's experience is an inspiration to all of us. No matter how difficult things seem, we *always* have choices. We can always decide what we think, how we feel and how we will act in a situation. The event does not make decisions for us. We either let it make our choices or make our own independent of it. As we increase our choices, our lives are enriched. This is the *Principle of Choice.*

There is a well-known saying, "Misery is optional." There's no reason for us to be unhappy if we don't want to be. What's done is done. Problems and mistakes of the past can never fully be erased but we can choose how we want to live our lives in the present. We have options and we can choose misery or happiness.

Perhaps we never knew we had a choice before. Those of us who discover that we have chosen misery for the first part of our lives can choose happiness for the next half. It doesn't fall in our laps. It takes effort and self-discipline. It takes a willingness to be open to new ways and a desire to grow. It takes hope and faith and some courage, too. But we always have options of how we experience life.

Good Luck? Bad Luck? Who Knows?

There is a Chinese story of an old farmer who had an old horse for tilling his fields. One day the horse escaped into the hills and when all the farmer's neighbors sympathized with the old man over his bad luck, the farmer replied, "Bad luck? Good luck? Who knows?"

A week later the horse returned with a herd of wild horses from the hills and this time the neighbors congratulated the farmer on his good luck. His reply again was, "Good luck? Bad luck? Who knows?"

Then when the farmer's son was attempting to tame one of the wild horses, he fell off its back and broke his leg. Everyone thought this very bad luck. Not the farmer, whose only reaction was, "Bad luck? Good luck? Who knows?"

Some weeks later the army marched into the village and conscripted every able-bodied youth they found there. When they saw the farmer's son with his broken leg, they let him off. Now was that good luck? Bad luck? Who knows?

From Anthony De Mello
Sadhana: A Way To God
(Doubleday, 1978).

The old farmer was a very wise man. Blessings often come to us in disguise. With patience we can see pain, loss and disappointment in their proper perspective. We can always find good in the bad when we look for it. Good and bad are all in the eye of the beholder. When we follow the Principles of Choice, we heal ourselves by changing the way we look at the world. We don't look through rose-colored glasses but we no longer see it as bleak and bewildering either. We have a better sense of balance between the two. We see more beauty than flaws, more hope than despair. We see blessings and constructive outcomes even in loss and disappointment.

We learn that it is we who can create a happy life, simply by the mental outlook we take. We know that on days when we are down and all hope seems to be gone, it is not the world but our mental attitude that needs changing. We know we cannot change the world, but we can change our view of it and thus erase the depressive and hopeless feelings. This grain of knowledge empowers us to change our whole existence from feeling helpless to being in charge. We can change our lenses to enthusiasm and fulfillment when our vision shows us dread and emptiness. Our lives are transformed with each new day as we change our lenses.

Figure 4.1. The Eye Of The Beholder

Beauty Is In The Eye Of The Beholder

Look at the drawing of the ugly old lady. She has a big nose, a scarf on her head, and her long chin is buried in her fur coat. Look at the drawing closely and try to figure out why she is so sad and unhappy.

I just defined your perception of this situation. Actually, I deliberately distorted your reality. Let's say I just staged you in an addictive-thinking situation because I influenced your perception of an event in a specific direction.

Perceptual psychologists have presented the ambiguous drawing of the young/old woman to many research subjects. Given the expectancy that they would see an old woman, subjects indeed did find the old woman's face before the young woman's face. Told that they would be shown the face of a young woman, subjects tended to see the young woman's face first and often had difficulty seeing the image of the old lady.

The Principle of Choice requires that you go back and re-examine the drawing in a new light. This time as you look at the drawing in a new way, you can see a beautiful young woman. The old woman's eye becomes the young woman's ear. The old woman's nose becomes the young woman's jawbone. The old woman's mouth is the young woman's necklace. Now you can look at the same picture and see an entirely different image.

Such is life. We always have the choice to re-examine our lives and reinterpret what we see. We can look at the good or the bad, the happiness or unhappiness, the success or failure. We can perceive our early lives as roadblocks and let them stand in our way. Or we can perceive them as stepping stones that will lead us to personal growth and fulfillment. Having filtered our lives up until now through the negative lenses of the past, we may need to train our eyes, ears and other senses to look for the beauty, joy, fun and happiness in life. What meaning can you find in your own painful past? I challenge you now to start looking at your life in a different way, from different angles, in fresh and new ways as never before. Your life will transform itself as you see things that were always there that you never noticed.

Cracks In The Pavement

When he first set foot into the foreign country, the tourist was awestruck by the beauty and cultural diversity. But after a week, he was fed up with what he saw. The uniqueness of the architecture was marred by the graffiti which he hadn't noticed before. The beauty of the towns and countryside soured as he began to pay attention to garbage in the river and cracks in the pavement.

Many times as an experience becomes familiar to us, we lose the fresh outlook we once had. Too few of us keep the enthusiasm we began our jobs with or the exhilaration we had when we started a family. Turning dislikes into preferences and negativity into positiveness can literally transform our mental outlook.

If we could view our lives through the fresh eyes of a foreigner, would we see the drudgery of another day's work or the excitement of what we do? Would we zip through the day with our heads stuck in computers or newspapers or would we hold conversations with the fascinating people with whom we come into contact? Would we yell and scream at the ones we love the most or forgive and love them as they are without trying to change them?

When we live each day as if it's our first, our lives are transformed. We get a deeper appreciation for who we are and for what we have. We gain a stronger bond for co-workers and loved ones who perhaps we take for granted. Let's ask ourselves, "Do we look for cracks in the pavement or pay attention to where the road takes us?"

Acting Versus Reacting

Many of us have spent a great deal of our lives being angry at store clerks, angry because their lines move too slowly, they never give us eye contact or because they are cold and indifferent. Actually I have come to realize that clerks are great dumping grounds for the public to deposit their addictive waste. Many times we are poised for them to say one cross word or to arch one eyebrow in the wrong direction. Then we pounce!

I include myself here. On regular visits to my local pharmacy, I encounter a clerk who has an unfriendly business-as-usual air about her. She never looks at me. When I smile and ask, "How are you today?" she doesn't respond. She literally snatches my prescription out of my hand. She still hasn't looked at me. And she walks away. My past reactions have been to lash out at her, which only makes her angry at me and me angrier at her. On some days I would alter my approach to "get her." When she'd snatch the prescription, I'd clench it tightly to make it harder for her to take. That would get her attention to make her look at me. It still seemed to annoy her and her annoyance further irritated me. We were both caught in a negative cycle of reactions which threw us out of charge of our lives.

Some of us glide through life reacting to life's random events through stimulus-response like rats in a maze. We respond in predictable ways without thinking about our choices. Our spouse, lover or roommate curses us and we curse back. A co-worker makes a disparaging remark, and we return the insult. A neighbor calls us an ugly name and we return the childish comment.

Healing teaches us to *act* with the gift of human reasoning, not to *react* like rats in a maze. We act when we use our new ways of thinking to make choices about how we behave. We react when we respond in predictable ways without conscious choice. Through reacting we are controlled by people and events. When we think and then act, we make conscious choices that put us in charge of our lives. A kind word diffuses a sour attitude. Calm in the face of hysteria has a soothing effect. Compliments reverse aspersions. In each case our behavior turns the tone of the situation completely around.

Once I began to realize that I had some say-so over my actions, I began to make more conscious choices about how I wished to think, feel and behave in all situations. One day when the pharmacy clerk persisted in her usual obstinate behavior, I smiled and asked, "How are you today?" She kept her eyes focused on the cash register and said nothing. I smiled and repeated, "How are you today?" She gruffly commented, "I'm fine," still not making eye contact and dumping the change into my hand. I continued to smile and walked away.

Changing the clerk's behavior was no longer my goal. Instead I focused on changing *my* behavior by untangling myself from the addictive interaction and choosing my actions — regardless of hers. Whether I felt good or bad that day did not depend on the sales clerk being nice to me. If I wanted to enjoy my day, it was up to me to enjoy it, regardless of the circumstances in which I found myself. Rather than getting caught in her swirl of addictive behaviors, I stood back and let her be. But most importantly I chose not to participate in the addictive interactions. Whether she yelled at me, ignored me or smiled at me no longer mattered because my behavior would be the same regardless. I learned that I have the power to act consistently with my own thoughts and feelings no matter how the situation bends and sways.

We can become emotionally paralyzed from life's problems. We feel powerless to do anything about them. We don't know which direction to move and are too immobile to make a move anyway. So we just mope around, moaning about how terrible things are and hoping they will improve. But situations do not get better on their own. We do not get something for nothing. Only self-action can change the negative course of our lives.

Maximizing Our Choices

Choice. It's one of the greatest words ever created. Think about it. It's a wonderful resource, and all of us have it available to us. It's up to each and every one of us to create the kind of life we want. The one thing no one can take away from us is the power of choice, no matter how hopeless our lives seem. No matter how horrendous our yesterdays, we can *choose* to transform them into happy and fulfilling todays and tomorrows. Few of us realize that we have an abundance of choices, and most of us do not know how to exercise them. Increasing choices available to us can transform our lives.

We can spend the rest of our lives agonizing over our addictive childhoods. Or we can use the unfortunate experiences as opportunities to change our lives and improve the quality.

Many of us choose to continue living in misery and bemoaning the horrible things that happened to us. We fault our addictive pasts as the reasons for our discontent. But we don't have to. If we want to get somewhere, we don't sit down. We take action and move. We take the path that is open to us. Spiritual growth often means leaving ourselves vulnerable, facing the risk of criticism and going against the fear.

Healing comes from action, not lethargy. Nothing ventured, nothing gained. Setting boundaries, taking risks, making choices, going with the fear, being optimistic — all are healing actions. We can risk being called "silly," being contradicted or being criticized but the risk makes us stronger. We can dare to heal ourselves by taking a new course of action. Take a new approach to solving old problems. Stop using old ways that don't work. Stop going back to the same people for the same rejections.

If something's not working, do something about it. If that doesn't work, do something else. Persist with another course of action, until eventually you solve your problem. Eliminate sameness and welcome change in your life.

If we could look at the way we live under a microscope, we would see how we put limits on our lives. We sometimes unintentionally limit ourselves out of a need for security. The more choices we have in life, the scarier it can be. So we eliminate choices by patronizing the same restaurants, holding the same jobs, following the same daily routines, and keeping the same close-knit friends.

Sameness limits our lives and growth as human beings.

We can eliminate sameness from our lives by getting out of the rut in which we find ourselves. We can take a different route home from work, eat lunch with new people at work whom we don't know as well, or face a new challenge that previously frightened us. By eliminating sameness, we eliminate boredom and roadblocks to personal growth. We open ourselves to new experiences and transform our old realities. We can choose one thing to do differently, no matter how small, that we have never done before. Then we can stand back and watch ourselves grow from this new experience.

Rediscovering Your Life

It is easy to become bored with the everyday monotony of our lives. The thrill and wonder are gone. We've seen and done it all. Life is no longer stimulating. Is that all there is?

These are only thoughts. These mental outlooks can be changed, and along with this change, come different feelings and a renewed outlook on life. We find beauty in the ordinary, elegance in the simple, wisdom in the shallow and excitement in the dull.

All of us have the power to change our views of ourselves and the daily world we live in. You can begin to exercise that power now. You can rediscover the world that you have lived in for so long and have taken for granted or ignored.

The next time you go to work, pretend that you have entered your workplace for the very first time. Look at people and places around you as if you are seeing and appreciating them for the first time. Notice what hangs on the walls, smell the flowers on someone's desk, see the color of the blouse or jacket a colleague is wearing, pay attention to the colors of the floor or the architecture of the buildings on the same street. Be mindful of the eyes of a co-worker, subordinate or boss. Look into their eyes and behind their eyes and see their gentle spirit.

When you try this technique, you will discover a world that has always been open to you, but you have never seen before. We must continue to look at everything we do in a different way and just as we see it differently, we change our outlook again.

How Are You Living Your Life?

Think of three things you like to do that make you happiest. Write them down in the blanks below. Now think of the last time you did each one. Was it a day ago, a week ago, a month ago or years ago? Beneath each favorite thing, put how long it's been since you've done it. What does this information tell you about how you're living your life? Did you have trouble even thinking of three favorite things? Are you doing the things you want to do in your life? Or are you living your life for someone else? All of us are making choices every moment of our lives, and we can become more aware of and exercise these choices more often.

First Favorite Thing: _____

_____

Last Time I Did It: _____

_____

Second Favorite Thing: _____

_____

Last Time I Did It: _____

_____

Third Favorite Thing: _____

_____

Last Time I Did It: _____

_____

What This Information Tells Me About How I'm Living My Life: _____

_____

_____

_____

_____

CHAPTER 5

Nature does abhor a vacuum, and when you begin moving out of your life what you do not want, you automatically are making way for what you do want.

Catherine Ponder

The Principle Of Vacuum

Getting rid of addictive thoughts and feelings clears a space for us to receive healing and happiness in our lives.

I attribute my own recovery, in large part, to the Principle of Vacuum. It began in the course of my Jamaican trip as I lay on the beach, reading about the Principle of Vacuum — how harboring negative thoughts and feelings leaves no room for prosperity and positive abundance to move into our lives. This principle says that we must make room for the positive by letting go of the negative.

An affirmation in that book by Catherine Ponder started change in my life. I visualized all the hostility that I had been carrying around suddenly evaporating from my body . . . like steam off a hot street after a summer rain. As I saw all these thoughts and feelings leaving my body, I began to actually feel lighter and less burdened. When I opened my eyes, a Jamaican man shimmied up a coconut palm tree, cracked open a coconut and offered me half to drink. Asking for nothing in return, he smiled and walked away. Good immediately began to flow into my life from that day forward.

The nightmares subsided, I felt an inner calm that I had never experienced before and I slept like a baby. I began to think positive thoughts about the old relationship, wishing harm to no one. During the next month a cornucopia of positive events poured into my life. I received more money than ever before. Healthier relationships came my way.

I am convinced that these changes resulted from the release of antagonistic thoughts and feelings, which formed a vacuum in my mind and heart. This vacuum cleared a space for me to establish more positive feelings, behaviors and mental outlook. I also am convinced, as a result of that experience, that forgiveness affirmations and meditations are keys to personal happiness.

The point of this story is that for the first time ever, I realized there was something I could do to change my life. I realized that no matter how dismal things appear to be, I don't have to be a victim of life. I cannot control everything that happens to me, but I can always take charge of what I will think, feel and do under every circumstance. Forming a vacuum became a concrete and simple technique that transformed my life.

As I continued in recovery, I learned that "Let go and let God" was a similar idea and that what I had done on the beach was to give up control and let life events take their own natural course. Another way of putting it is that I had stepped out of my own way so that I could live more fully. Later I would learn that this is a fundamental teaching in The 12 Steps . . . of admitting our powerlessness and turning our self-will and our lives over to a Higher Power.

In a nutshell the Principle of Vacuum says that you must get rid of what you don't want in your life in order to make room for better to enter. On a metaphysical level, nature abhors a vacuum and will quickly fill one up.

Suppose you want money for a new wardrobe but your closets are overflowing with old clothes. The money will not manifest itself until you get rid of the old clothes that are tattered and torn and no longer fit. By doing so, you create a vacuum and open the way for the money and new wardrobe to come into your life.

Suppose you want healthier relationships, but your life is crowded with unhealthy friends. You must first let go of the unhealthy relationships that no longer feel right to make room for healthier people to enter your life.

Suppose you want a happier life altogether, but your mind is cluttered with old addictive thought patterns that no longer serve the happy lifestyle you seek. You must evacuate the addictive thought patterns to make room for new healing ways of thinking and living. The Principle of Vacuum is about letting go of the old, the familiar and the things, people and attitudes that you have outgrown. Once you form the vacuum, you create an open current for health, prosperity and happiness to fill your life.

Holding On For Dear Life

Ruth's best friend had no place to go. So Ruth, being a generous and kind soul, invited her friend to come live with her, as well as Ruth's husband of 25 years and their three children. During the course of the next year Ruth kept house, did all the cooking and remained a good mother and wife. She was delighted that her best friend could become part of her family. But the generous offer turned sour when Ruth discovered that her friend and her husband had been having an affair for several months. Her husband and her best friend moved away together and were eventually married. Ruth was left with an emptiness that was quickly filled with bitterness, resentment, anger and hate for two people who had been her closest allies. Holding on to those negative feelings actually caused Ruth more pain and hurt than the people they were directed toward. Ruth's husband and friend, who were not hurt at all by the stored feelings, had begun a happy new life in another city. Constantly unhappy, lonely and angry toward others, Ruth suffered the emotional and physical consequences of carrying these stored feelings for years.

Many of us are more accustomed to holding on to what we want than we are of letting it go. Our way of life teaches us to possess rather than give, not only with material things but with feelings as well. If we get something, we win. If we give up something, we lose. So we are more likely to possess, own, accumulate, cling and take than we are to give up and let go.

The tale of *Silas Marner* is a good example of how hoarding money keeps us poverty-stricken because it closes us down. Spending it wisely or making donations to worthy causes creates a vacuum that opens a channel for prosperity to flow back. As good comes to us, we must let go of it in order to keep it. Letting it go maintains a vacuum for more to enter. We cannot hoard prosperity or happiness like we would cage an animal. The negative traits of hoarding, possessing and selfishness block the channels of receptivity. Only by letting go of greedy and selfish ways can our spiritual progress continue to flow. "Go with the flow" literally means tapping into the currents of energy that move and flow around us and riding these magnetic waves in the direction they're going.

Why Do We Cling To Our Painful Memories?

Ruth couldn't have her husband, but she could have her anger and bitterness toward him. Ruth felt that if she gave that up, too, she would have lost everything. With her negative emotions she felt that at least she would have something to hold on to. This is addictive thinking.

We become addicted to holding on to old resentments because we get emotional satisfaction from them. We think we need them. We don't want to let go. Much of the time we are afraid to let the addictive thoughts go. We're afraid that if we give up our grudges and resentments, we will unleash a groundswell of emotions like a bursting dam. We're afraid we can never stop crying. Or we're afraid of our own anger.

Perhaps our biggest fear is that if we give up old addictive thoughts and feelings, there will be nothing left of us. The truth is that we do ourselves more harm by not giving up addictive thinking. It keeps us preoccupied and obsessed with the negative situation. It keeps us stuck in the past and blocks our spiritual flow so that nothing moves out and nothing moves in. Harboring vengeance and hatred hurts no one but ourselves. It keeps us emotionally imprisoned with thoughts and feelings that are under the control of our perpetrators. It eats away at us like a disease. It clouds our perceptions of situations and other people. It keeps our thinking distorted and our thoughts always focused on the negative.

Perhaps a parent abused us. A co-worker ridiculed us at the office for some mistake. Or a loved one humiliated us in front of other family members. We can still feel the stinging hurt. The memories are as fresh as yesterday. The pain is so heavy our heart aches.

What purpose does hanging on to old resentments serve? We clutch them out of revenge because hanging on to hate is our only means of retaliation. It is our way of punishing the ones who hurt us. Or we may hold on to the old emotions because we feel sorry for ourselves. Anger and malice are heavy items to carry. Bearing their burden is like carrying a ton weight around. It takes a lot of energy away from us to bear them day in and day out. It makes us tired, frustrated and irritable. We don't have strength for the beauty of recovery. There's no room left for life's positive side but carrying a chip on our shoulder only hurts *us*. It weighs us down. It keeps us in the trenches of spiritual impoverishment.

Physician Bernie Siegel says that we store our childhoods inside our bodies and that once we're grown, our body collects the bill. Our addictive thoughts can lead to life-threatening illnesses because they cause a chemical reaction inside our bodies. Negative thoughts are transformed into negative chemical reactions that manifest in serious physical illness. Siegel insists that if we don't get out these thoughts, they will give us a disease, make us overweight or in some way destroy us. He says that if we keep ignoring our needs, our bodies hear the message that we don't care about ourselves and it helps us die.

It doesn't take a genius to know that headaches, ulcers, palpitations, nausea and other physical symptoms often come from storage of our emotions. Unless we inventory our emotional stock and get rid of the damaged goods, the addictive thoughts and feelings will fester and eventually cause us great physical and mental harm.

Letting Go For Dear Life

The Principle of Vacuum is about releasing all the addictive thoughts and feelings that can do us harm — animosities, anger, fear, worry, jealousy, hurt, depression. As long as we act as a storehouse of addictive thoughts, we have no space for healing thoughts. We walk around angry or unhappy most of the time and don't even understand why. The one who clutches resentments will be consumed and destroyed by them.

Gary Zukav in his book, *The Seat Of The Soul*, proclaims that we have a multitude of different currents inside ourselves. He says we learn to experience the energy of our soul when our personality . . . "learns to value and to identify with those currents that generate creativity, healing and love, and to challenge and release those currents that create negativity, disharmony and violence." Love, compassion and wisdom are experiences of the soul. Releasing grudges, resentments and old hurts takes that weight off our shoulders, makes our burden lighter and raises us up from the depths to higher ground. We feel cleansed and renewed. Having released the old, we are now ready to receive the new. Letting go opens our spiritual channels and lets the negative flow out and the positive flow in.

There are many ways to evacuate your addictive thoughts and feelings. The essential point is to get the thoughts and feelings moving in an outward direction, instead of holding on to them. The following methods can help you express feelings in a healthy way and to evacuate addictive thoughts and feelings so that you can maintain your mental and physical health.

- Talking to a trusted friend or trained therapist helps get the flow moving out from the body, rather than in. Support groups, such as 12-Step programs, also help us talk out damaging thoughts and feelings in a caring atmosphere.

- Keeping a journal or diary, writing your thoughts down or talking them into a tape recorder gets the flow moving outward and away from you. This is especially valuable for those who feel the need for privacy.
- Employing any type of creative outlet, such as art, drama, music or poetry, can help you express and release unhealthy feelings in constructive ways.
- Venting strong feelings of rage through such constructive ways as pounding clay, batting a punching bag or hitting your bed moves them out of your body onto inanimate objects. It doesn't matter whether you cry them out, scream them out, bang them out or laugh them out, as long as you get them outside of yourself.
- Exercising in some form — such as running, aerobics, fast walking or sports activities — enables us to work out frustration, anger and other conflicting feelings.
- Using forgiveness affirmations and meditations is one of the most valuable ways of evacuating negative energy and creating a vacuum for positive energy flow.

Creating A Vacuum Through Forgiveness Affirmations

The major way to let go and unclog our emotional channels is through forgiveness. We can set ourselves free by forgiving the wrongdoer and ourselves and releasing the resentments one by one. Forgiveness forms a vacuum because we release addictive thoughts (negative and unhealthy ones) and give off healing thoughts in their place. The vacuum is immediately filled with a sense of freedom, peace and serenity.

"Why should Ruth forgive her husband and best friend?" you may explode. "That was an unforgivable thing they did to her!" To that I answer nothing is unforgivable. We don't condone what the husband and friend did, but they did nothing "to her." It is up to Ruth to decide for herself whether she will be *harmed* or *helped* by the incident. No one else makes that decision for her.

She can allow herself to be victimized and endure the pain and hardship. Or she can surmount the problem and become spiritually strengthened by it. Mourning her loss and forgiving her husband and friend enable her to rise above the problem. Creating a vacuum through forgiveness is done in the privacy of her heart for *her* benefit, not for *theirs*.

If Ruth holds on to her unforgiving ways, she harms herself through mental and physical self-abuse. But if she lets go of her negative thoughts and feelings, she follows an act of self-love and becomes the beneficiary of peace and serenity.

Forgiving others for the wrongs they have committed is the ultimate act of self-love.

Forgiveness rids us of hurt and frees us to make decisions about our actions rather than allowing the event to make the decision for us. Forgiveness strengthens and heals us because we think and feel for ourselves, independently of the painful situation. We make decisions about how we feel from situation to situation and day to day. We don't wait for other people or situations to make them for us.

Acts of forgiveness are done for our benefit, not for someone else's.

Part of letting go is forgiving yourself for carrying addictive thoughts and feelings and forgiving others for what they did . . . silently forgiving them for *your* benefit, regardless of whether they ever hear or accept your apology.

What grudges can you renounce that, through forgiveness of others and yourself, will heal your life? Think of any person toward whom you harbor negative feelings and be ready to let the feelings go for *your* sake.

A declaration by Catherine Ponder from her book, *The Dynamic Laws of Prosperity*, helped me let go of my resentments and create a vacuum of positive flow in my life. Repeat this affirmation as often as you need to and visualize the anger, hate, contempt and any other negative emotions evaporating from your body as you declare:

I fully and freely forgive you. I loose you and let you go. So far as I am concerned that incident between us is finished forever.
I do not wish to hurt you. I wish you no harm. I am free and you are free and all is well again between us.

You can practice this forgiveness affirmation for 15 minutes each day. Forgiving yourself or others creates the vacuum that will undam your resentments. If you have been self-critical or have criticized others, you can let go of blame. Think of anyone (including yourself) whom you have condemned, criticized or treated unkindly. Think of those whom you dislike, feel anger toward, resent or in any way feel out of harmony. Imagine them in your mind and declare the above affirmation over and over until you feel yourself cleansed. As you try these affirmations and learn to let go of the harmful feelings, you receive a feeling of joy and serenity that is unparalleled. Below are additional affirmations you can use to carry you through the day:

Today I release all resentments that I carry. My heart refills with love and forgiveness as the burden of resentment melts away.

I will inventory my feelings for old grudges and where they exist, I will let them go. As I give them up, I feel healed and further along the road of recovery. I am a happier and healthier person as a result.

Today I inventory old feelings and release the ones that I still clutch. I bury the hatchet once and for all and set myself free.

I ask for strength to practice forgiveness while maintaining my own sense of self-worth. Inspiration from my Higher Power helps me stand independent from the emotional situation like a giant oak.

I create an inner vacuum. I evacuate all the self-destructive thoughts and feelings that I have stored in my mind. I refill the vacuum with healthy thoughts and feelings to take the place of the unhealthy ones.

I will name all the self-destructive behaviors that I have harbored to survive my past. One by one I will let them go and replace them with healthier ways of thinking, feeling and being in the world.

Burying The Hatchet For Good

A word of caution about forgiveness. Sometimes we pretend to forgive but our heart isn't in it. We continue to mentally hang on to old anger, hurt and self-pity. Or we make a conspicuous display of martyrdom by forgiving the accused in a grandstand fashion.

Sidney Harris once said, "There's no point in burying a hatchet if you're going to put up a marker on the site." If our heart truly is not into forgiving and if we cannot release our addictive thoughts freely, forgiveness affirmations will not work. No vacuum will be formed and nothing better will replace the addictive thinking. But once we take an honest inventory of addictive thoughts and feelings and release the ones that we still clutch, we can bury the hatchet once and for all and set ourselves free.

The following exercise gives you hands-on experience in burying the hatchet for good — not only for past transgressions but for anything that will happen in the future. Think of someone toward whom you feel a lot of anger, hurt or resentment. This can be someone who did something you didn't like or someone who constantly arouses feelings in you simply for being "chronically who they are" — such as a parent who constantly puts you down or a spouse who always looks for the negative in everything.

Ask yourself if you are ready to forgive this person *entirely* and *completely*. Are you ready to forgive this person even for things he or she has yet to do or will continue to do? Remember that you must be willing to forgive that person *totally* for all past, present and future behaviors. Once you can truthfully answer yes, write down on a sheet of paper this person's name and what he or she did or does that arouses your strong feelings. Close your eyes and imagine yourself talking with that person. Visualize the person doing whatever it is that bothers you. Next, see yourself forgiving that person *totally* and *completely*. Get in touch with the feelings that come up and experience them.

After you feel true forgiveness in your heart, open your eyes. Tear the paper into tiny pieces and throw it into the trash bin. The next time the addictive voice inside reminds you of your negative feelings toward this person, repeat with your healing voice, "Thanks for sharing, but I've already forgiven him or her."

Creating Vacuum Through Meditation

We often hear that we can turn our will and problems over to a Higher Power. We may ask, "How do I turn off the neon sign?" or "Where do I begin to let go and create a vacuum?" What are the mechanics of giving up burdensome problems when they continue to haunt us? Meditations are useful techniques to train your mind to free its addictive ways of thinking. You can create an endless exodus of all the shame, worry, fear, hurt and any other addictive thoughts and feelings that crowd your mind and hold you back from living fully. As the self-abusive thoughts and feelings make a mass exodus, a waterfall of healing flows in and fills the void. You can use your own power of visualization to make this happen.

In a quiet and comfortable place, close your eyes and clear your mind of cluttered thoughts. After you are relaxed, visualize each problem that occupies your mind slowly leaving your body. See it evaporating through the top of your head and into the clouds. Image the negative thoughts and feelings gone and see the vacuum that you have made. Imagine that empty space being taken up by love, joy, beauty and any other healthy and healing images. Visualize these positive currents entering your head and filling your heart to the depths of your soul. At a later time when the negative thoughts compete for your attention, remind yourself that they are no longer yours. Continue this exercise as often as you need to evacuate and renew your spirit.

How To Get Rid Of Problems

Another way you can begin to shed troubled thoughts is to think about your three biggest worries (problems, fears) that stand in the way of your happiness. Now rank them in order from the biggest to the smallest. Then *visualize a huge sack, enough room in it for all the problems of the world* — all the things that keep you from happiness. Imagine yourself putting each of your worries, one by one, inside the sack. You see the problem disappearing as you put it into the bag. You tie the bag with string and see it bulging at the seams with your problems as they punch around inside. You lift the heavy bag with all your strength, carry it to the front door and set it outside on the doorstep.

The problems are no longer yours. They lie by the door waiting to be picked up along with the garbage. As you leave for the day, you look by the doorstep and notice that the bag is gone. All of the problems were collected by your Higher Power. You replace the heavy load with peace and serenity. Every time the neon tries to flash, you stop it by visualizing the bag bulging with your old problems. Today your troubles are in the hands of your Higher Power, and you put your thought and energy into other things that you can change.

CHAPTER 6

An optimist goes to the window every morning and says, 'Good morning, God.' The pessimist goes to the window and says, 'Good God, morning!'

Anonymous

The Principle Of Optimism

We can create a positive and happy life by taking an optimistic outlook and by looking on the positive side of situations, rather than the negative side.

A Fable: Finding Your Pony

Once upon a time there was a set of twin boys, age 12. Although identical in looks and genetics, the boys had totally opposite personalities. One twin always saw the positive side in every situation. The other boy was the most negative child one could imagine. Nothing was ever good enough. The negative child was critical and fault-finding of everything and everyone. In exasperation the parents consulted a psychiatrist who told them to capitalize on the twins' upcoming birthdays as a way to reverse their mental outlooks. He instructed the parents to spare no expense in buying the negative son the most wonderful and exciting toys and presents they could find. The positive son was to receive absolutely nothing. Instead the parents would take him into a room filled chest-high with manure.

The parents didn't feel comfortable about this approach but they reluctantly agreed. On the birthday the negative son was treated to a truckload of fabulous items. After two hours of unwrapping one expensive present after another, he commented, "Gee whiz, is this all I get?"

By now the parents were at their wits' end. The positive son had waited patiently for his turn and admired each of his brother's gifts, telling him how fortunate he was to have such wonderful presents. As the psychiatrist had instructed, the parents then took the positive son to a room filled with horse manure, shoved him in and closed the door.

After 30 minutes of fretting and worrying about how the son was doing, the parents threw open the door and called desperately to their son. The child was shoveling as hard and fast as he could, and his head was barely visible above the mountain of manure. Continuing to shovel frantically, the son smiled and exclaimed, "Gee, thanks, Mom and Dad! I know there's got to be a pony in here somewhere!"

The Principle of Optimism is about finding the pony. Many of us, being such negative thinkers, see only the manure. We were directly or indirectly told from a young age that something is wrong with us; we could never do anything right. For a lifetime we believed the illusion. We believed that we were shameful, unattractive and second-rate. We believed that the world is full of hardships, unhappiness and pain. We believed that life contains mostly catastrophe, misery and suffering. We learned these addictive beliefs from the views of those around us and from the reflections of their negative inner selves. We looked into their negative mirrors and learned to look at life and ourselves in the same addictive way. Our negative looking glass defined who we were; and now we spread, either through words or examples, these addictive thoughts to others — our children, colleagues, spouses and friends.

Addictive Chitchat

Addictive messages blink in our troubled minds like a neon sign. We stew over mistakes we make, worry about things we cannot control and expect the worst in each situation. In addictive homes parents often humiliate their kids or call them names. After hearing, "Can't you do anything right?" or "You're always getting into trouble" or "You're such a failure," children start to believe and feel that they are in fact unworthy.

Glenda remembered an aunt holding her firmly by the shoulders and looking her squarely in the eyes. The aunt pounded into her seven-year-old brain, "You're a redhead. You can *never* wear red. You look awful in red! It makes you look silly. You look like a firetruck with your red hair!" This addictive message dominated Glenda's thinking and behavior for 40 years, and she spent her entire life afraid to wear red. Glenda had molded her thoughts, feelings and behaviors around her aunt's perception. Now at 47, although she understands that her aunt's perception was not necessarily shared by everyone, Glenda still feels uncomfortable wearing red clothing.

In childhood we internalize messages about ourselves that we get from adults. These messages — true or untrue — become our reality. In adulthood the messages continue to remind us of who we are through mental chitchat. Much of what we think and do is still dictated by our refusal to let go of inner dialogue. Addictive thoughts, acquired in childhood, still drive us as adults and damage our self-worth.

As I mentioned before, the typical morning wakeup call that Joe got from his father was, "Get your lazy ass out of bed!" That addictive thought pierced his young brain. He was lazy, no good, thus unworthy. He spent the majority of his adult life trying to prove his self-worth through his own work addiction that almost killed him.

"I'm unworthy" is a message he gave himself regularly so that he continued to push to succeed until he could feel worthy. Other addictive messages are "I'll never make it," "Nothing I do is ever good enough," "I can't do it," "I'm too short," "I'm too tall," "I'm too thin," "I'm too fat," "I'm too dumb." The list is endless.

How pessimistic are you? The box contains a self-test to help you think about the addictive messages you send

How Pessimistic Are You?

Ask yourself how strongly you agree or dis-agree with the following statements. Then write in the appropriate number.

> 1 = strongly disagree
> 2 = disagree
> 3 = agree
> 4 = strongly agree

____ 1. Life is full of problems.

____ 2. Always assume people will do you in.

____ 3. I can't meet most challenges that I face.

____ 4. Nothing I ever do is good enough.

____ 5. Whatever can go wrong will go wrong.

____ 6. I'm a born loser.

____ 7. I can't help the way I am.

____ 8. Trouble follows me everywhere I go.

____ 9. I don't like the way I look.

____ 10. I'm not a very worthy person.

____ TOTAL SCORE

SCORING: Add the numbers in the blanks. Put your total score in the space at the bottom.

If your score is . . .

> 10 to 20, you are not pessimistic.
> 21 to 29, you are mildly pessimistic.
> 30 to 40, you are highly pessimistic.

to yourself. Giving up these addictive beliefs about yourself and wiping the slate clean starts the healing process.

Selecting The Negative

As adults many of us continue wearing the addictive
sunglasses of our past. Psychiatrist David Burns says that
our bad feelings about ourselves, our relationships and
the world at large come from negative and pessimistic
thoughts. We unconsciously filter the positive aspects of
our lives and allow only negative aspects to enter. Our
addictive thinking tells us that nothing we ever do is good
enough. Our flaws always stand out from the shine.

We get a bronze medal, but we *should* have won the gold.
We make a 98 on an exam and condemn ourselves for not
making 100. We receive the promotion but it's still not high
enough up the corporate ladder. We made salesperson of
the month but still didn't break the all-time sales record.

Defeated attitudes beget defeated lives. As long as we
think addictively, we stay stuck in defeat, and we will
experience defeat. When we are ready to acknowledge
our successes, we become successful and we heal.

This bad habit of selecting the negative over the positive
eventually leads us to believe that everything is negative.

A woman ordering dinner in a four-star restaurant
came across "soup du jour" on the menu. "Soup du jour,"
she moaned to her companion. "I don't recommend it. I
had it one time at another restaurant and it was terrible!"

This is an example of how negative thinking can lead
to rejecting an entire class of items (be it people, food or
whatever) based on one isolated experience. Pessimism
causes us to generalize one event to include the whole
class of events. The point is that we limit our choices by
closing ourselves off to the range of possibilities. We
close our minds to a large portion of what we allow to
enter our lives.

We look at the dark side of life, rather than the bright
side. Although there are two sides, we virtually close off
joy, beauty and happiness. It is easy to see and accept the

negative side of life. Incompetence, insensitivity and self-ishness are easy to spot. We become pessimistic and cynical. Even when everything is going our way, we're depressed and unhappy and cannot figure out why. Often we're waiting for the ax to fall because if we get too comfortable with the good, we won't be prepared for the bad. So our addictive thinking keeps us stuck in addictive living and we think that only bad things can happen to us.

Collecting Evidence

Too few of us obey the Principle of Optimism. Instead we carry a magnifying glass, looking for flaws and defects. We are critical of others and berate ourselves. We wage war on ourselves and see an enemy in everyone we meet. We complain, condemn and judge others. We moan about our misery and blame someone else for our despair. We are more comfortable living the life of an underdog than we are living on top.

Those of us with pessimistic mindsets collect evidence that, in fact, matches our negative beliefs about ourselves. Essentially we make present experiences coincide with our addictive thinking. We verify our unworthiness by unconsciously proving how inadequate we really are. When incoming feedback from people around us conflicts with our perceptions of ourselves, we change it to fit our pessimistic attitudes and feelings. In other words we turn positive situations into negative ones.

Positive evidence coming through our negative lenses doesn't fit with our addictive views. So we turn this evidence around, discount it, ignore it, downplay it or in some way distort it so that it fits with our idea of who we are. When we have positive experiences, we tell ourselves it was just an accident. When we have negative experiences, we tell ourselves that this is living proof of how inadequate we are. We let compliments, for example, sail over our heads when we could embrace them and take them into our hearts.

We blush when someone praises us. We feel discomfort when we are applauded for a kind deed. We feel awkward when someone compliments us on how we look. Compliments are sometimes hard to accept, especially when we cannot acknowledge the good in ourselves. We often find it easier to accept negative comments and put-downs because they more closely match our self-images. Many of us, because we are so used to criticism, feel more comfort with it than praise.

A colleague of mine takes compliments and turns them into insults against herself or others. When someone told her how nice her hair looked, she'd say, "Are you kidding? It looks like a mop!" When friends complimented her on her work, she'd snap, "Stop making of fun of what I did. I know it's not as good as yours but I'm doing the best I can."

This woman, the product of a dysfunctional family, saw only the worst in herself and in everyone else. She had few friends because of her sour attitude. Her relationships with men were short-lived because she found their weak spots and ripped them to shreds. Once a small group of neighbors commented on the kindness of a man who had just moved into the neighborhood. She interrupted the conversation and turned it around. "I hate him. He's such a wimp!" she loudly exclaimed. "He has no backbone at all. I don't think he's kind. I think he's a spineless jerk!"

As she lambasted the man, the mood of the group changed. It was as if a dark cloud hovered above. Without a word, the other neighbors started to distance themselves from the negative woman and in seconds the group had disbanded. People like the negative woman are often said to be poison, because they pollute the tone of a whole group.

Addictive thinkers can lower morale on the job and can be divisive in social gatherings because they dump their addictive waste on everyone else. Their negative energy can be so strong sometimes that others can feel it filtering into the air. Feeling discomfort from the negative contamination, we unconsciously distance ourselves from the addictive person. It is in this way that negative thinking creates negative reality. The woman's sour attitude turned the other neighbors against her, and in so doing created more negative experiences for herself.

We are not always aware that we go about our days collecting evidence of our low self-worth like butterflies in a net. At the end of the day we sort and classify our collection. We assemble and reassemble negative comments, defeats and mistakes as we would arrange dried insects on a board. We examine our collection of evidence inside out, upside down and right side up. We replay every comment and every negative feeling.

But what about the ones that got away? Had we aimed our net in another direction, we would have a collection of compliments, successes and joys to sort and classify too. We could spend the rest of the day examining these specimens from every possible angle too. But we are not used to collecting items that add to our self-worth.

Ask yourself what kinds of evidence about yourself you collect during a day. Do you focus on the all-too-familiar negative? Or do you hold out for the rare positive feedback that gives you greater value?

Self-Sabotage

One of the chief ways we sabotage ourselves is to set our standards so high that we are bound to fail. We set ourselves up for failure by comparing ourselves to the best of everything in every category. We must be smart like Einstein, be creative like Leonardo da Vinci, be sensitive like Mother Theresa, be witty like Joan Rivers, be rich like Donald Trump, play tennis like Boris Becker, have the sex appeal of Paul Newman.

We are bound to fall short of our standards and experience self-devaluation. Addictive thinking leads to telescopic thinking because we zero in on our defeats. Even if we excel in three out of four areas, we ignore the three areas of achievement and focus on the one in which we fall short. We berate ourselves and think of ourselves as failures, although we may be perceived as outstanding by others. We continue to overlook our accomplishments and positive actions because we are focused on the area where we fall short. Through such superhuman standards we send ourselves addictive messages with self-criticism and self-contempt.

"That was a stupid thing to do" or "I just can't seem to do anything right" are familiar rings to the ears of addictive thinkers. We continue to have addictive thoughts and feelings, as well as addictive relationships, and we pass our addictive thinking on to those with whom we live, work and play.

Equal Time

The Principle of Optimism says, "Make peace with yourself. You no longer need addictive thoughts because they don't fit your new healing life." Unhealthy thought patterns are replaced by healthy ones. The Principle of Optimism teaches us that, like coins, life has two sides. Obeying this Principle means giving the positive equal time with the negative. We rephrase negative thoughts into positive ones to make our lives healthier and happier. We balance our lives with beauty, acceptance, peace, friendship, gratitude, responsibility, happiness and goodness. We don't have to look far. The positive aspects in life, although often shadowy figures, are all around us. We're so unaccustomed to seeing them that we have to look harder for them.

At 40 years of age, those of us who view our lives with despair think of life as half over. But optimistic eyes view it as another exciting half to go. We make out of life what we want. When we enter a rose garden, we can be repelled by the thorns or drawn by the beauty and fragrance of the flowers. When we hear the weather forecast of 50 percent chance of rain, we can remind ourselves that there's also a 50 percent chance that it will not rain.

The Principle of Optimism teaches us to look for the other positive 50 percent of life that has been perceptually unavailable to us. Obeying this principle requires that we love ourselves and see ourselves truthfully. Doing this means magnifying our own good in proportion to our downfalls and forgiving ourselves for the mistakes we make. Once we begin to see ourselves as we really are, we discover that we are not nearly as horrible as we had thought.

Seeing ourselves truthfully includes acknowledging and affirming all the good things about ourselves. Once we accept ourselves truthfully, we can accept those compliments that used to sail over our heads. We can take them into our hearts without false pride or false modesty. Learning to accept compliments is a way of learning the truth about ourselves.

The Principle of Optimism teaches us to "dwell on happiness" rather than "dwell on despair." Who has time to concentrate on being happy when we have so much pain to bear and so many problems to solve? How can we dwell on happiness when we have so much strife at work and disharmony at home? We have the choice of where we want to put our thoughts. Ignoring problems won't make them go away, but we can decide that we will give happiness equal time with despair. Both sorrow and happiness are part of life. The dualities of joy and sadness, hate and love, right and wrong, good and evil — all are part of life's total package.

Life is only as dreary as we let it become. By dwelling on joy, happiness, love and good, we give the other 50 percent equal time. And we treat ourselves to a more balanced, self-satisfying experience of life. Doesn't it make more sense to start the day with optimism rather than despair, helping rather than withholding, with a smile instead of a frown? We may feel mournful and discouraged inside. But that doesn't mean we have to take the mournful route. Even when we feel down, we can take the uplifting path. When we choose a path of light over one of darkness, we transform our lives.

Finding The Optimistic Side Of Me

Using a second hand, time yourself on this exercise. List five positive traits about yourself that you can describe in one word:

1.
2.
3.
4.
5.

How long did it take? Now list five negative traits about yourself that you can describe in one word below:

1.
2.
3.
4.
5.

How long did it take? Compare the time it took to list the positive traits with the time it took to list the negative ones. Almost always it is quicker to name five negative things than five positive things because the negative is what has been mirrored to us. It's easier to believe the negative than the positive. We wear it more comfortably because that's what we've always known. This is addictive thinking. Once you can find the positive side of yourself as quickly as you can find the negative side, you know the Principle of Optimism is working for you.

"Should" On Me

Many of us are not aware of it, but overuse of the word "should" makes us feel and think in pessimistic ways about ourselves and breaks the Principle of Optimism. This is an exercise from Louise Hay. Name some things you "should" have done today or yesterday or last week. Try to think of at least three. Write them down. One man's "shoulds" looked like this:

1. *I should have finished that report on Friday.*
2. *I should have been more sympathetic to her problem.*
3. *I should have invited her to the party.*

Now look at how this man is choosing to make himself feel shameful and guilty for his actions. If we were to ask him why he "should" have done those things, he would answer that his teachers always told him to finish what he started or his parents pounded into his brain that he should be sensitive to other people. "Shoulds" are often shame-based addictive messages drilled into our minds at an early age. They are barriers to our self-esteem.

We can turn those shame-based messages around by replacing the word "should" with "could:"

1. *I could have finished that report on Friday.*
2. *I could have been more sympathetic to her problem.*
3. *I could have invited her to the party.*

Now look at your list of "shoulds." Substitute the word "could" for each of your "shoulds" and notice how it changes the meaning of your statements and thus the messages you send to yourself. Rather than filling ourselves with pessimism and shame, we can begin to tell ourselves that we have a choice and that we may have simply chosen not to exercise that choice. Shame and guilt vanish, we become more optimistic and we send ourselves healthier and more balanced affirmations.

Erasing Old Chitchat

Louise Hay once said, "Part of self-acceptance is releasing other people's opinions." How can you turn off the neon sign that blinks addictive signals in your brain? What are the mechanics of turning pessimism into optimism? In a word . . . *practice.*

The following chart can help you do just that. For every *addictive message* I have supplied a *healing message*.

Addictive Messages	Healing Messages
"I want to be loved by everyone."	"It would be nice to be loved by everyone, but that is unrealistic. My worth doesn't depend on everyone liking me."
"I must be thoroughly competent in all things I do."	"Trying to be outstanding in just one task is difficult. Achievements do not determine my worth."
"Other people upset me."	"Sometimes I let other people upset me."
"My unhappiness is usually caused by events and people over which I have no control."	"I can take charge of my life by choosing my thoughts, feelings and actions."
"I am responsible for the happiness in my family."	"I am responsible for my behavior and happiness while others are responsible for their behavior and happiness."
"I cannot help the way I am."	"It is up to me to change the things I can that keep my life from working."
"My way is the best way."	"There are many ways to get something done. Mine is only one way. I am willing to listen and negotiate."
"Things have to be perfect for me to be happy."	"Life is uncertain and people, myself included, are not perfect."

"My destiny is set."

"Life is full of pain and misery."

"Anything is possible. I take responsibility for my future."

"Life is full of whatever I choose it to be."

Every time you catch yourself sending an addictive message, you can intercept it and substitute a healing message in its place. After a period of dedicated practice you will begin to see a difference in your ability to think and feel more positively about yourself. As a beginning exercise, substitute an optimistic statement for each of the 10 pessimistic statements in the box on page 78. Say each optimistic message to yourself two or three times.

During the next week, be on the lookout for addictive chitchat that you have with yourself. Keep track of these negative statements by writing them in a daily log without censorship. At the end of the week look over your list. Star the ones that occur more than once. You may be surprised at how often you tell yourself how stupid or unworthy you are. These are the unhealthy messages that you live by. They govern your feelings, thoughts and behaviors. They tell you what you think of yourself, reflect how you behave and even may indicate how others perceive you. They prevent your life from working the way you want it to.

Beside every addictive thought you listed for the week, substitute a healing message. Work with the messages that you most often send yourself first. Practice sending the healing thoughts to yourself as often as you can during the day: In the morning as you look in the mirror, on the way to work, while waiting in a line or before falling asleep at night. You have begun to obey the Principle of Optimism. Practicing this exercise enough will start positive changes and your life will begin to heal.

Pep Talks

Whether you're taking a test, making a speech, starting a new job or struggling with parenthood, doubt and lack of confidence can flood your mind. You might tell yourself, "I can't do this. I might as well give up." Engaging in such addictive thinking sets you up for needless failure. When you have these negative feelings always ask, "What would I say to my best friend or child if they thought they couldn't do something?" You wouldn't say, "Of course you can't do it. You might as well give up." Your confidence in their ability would lead you to encourage them through pep talks. Once we love ourselves enough to be our own best friend, we'll give ourselves that same encouragement that we give to others. Pep talks bring self-reassurance and ultimate success. Tell yourself, "Yes, I can do this. And I can do it well."

Keep sending yourself positive, encouraging messages. Image the best of outcomes, instead of the worst. Give yourself pep talks. Encourage yourself just as you do your best friend. Tell yourself, "I can do whatever I set my mind to do." Use a mirror. Look at yourself and bombard yourself with the truth: "You can do anything you can think of, and you can do it well."

Gratitude: Selecting The Positive

A woman took a hard-earned vacation to a Florida resort. During the entire trip she complained of the sweltering heat, the grim-faced people and the long lines. Everything was far too expensive. The music, she complained, sounded like a truckload of socket wrenches being dumped on a radiator. All she wanted was a chair and an air conditioner.

She was miserable the entire time until her last day at the resort. Just beyond the scent of gardenias and jasmine, the draperies of a window opened wide and she saw it: a woman in an iron lung. She paused for a moment, then walked in silence back into the world of glaring sunlight, crowds and sore feet — this time with no complaints.

Sometimes we let the trivial and petty things in life detract us from what is most important, and it may take a jolt to realize how truly fortunate we are. The day-to-day annoyances we complain about are suddenly trivial when we face a major catastrophe. We gripe and complain about minor inconveniences when our lives are already rich and full. Counting our blessings and being grateful for all that we have turns pessimism into optimism. Gratitude helps us see the glass as half full, instead of half empty. Gratitude helps us see the good in everything that comes our way. We find enlightenment in misunderstanding, acceptance in disappointment and understanding in confusion.

The children need a new pair of shoes, the house needs a new roof and the dishwasher is broken. The car is in the shop, we didn't get the raise we expected, we're behind with the bills and we're overworked. On the other hand, our family has their health, we have plenty of food on the table, we have each other, we're alive and we have this beautiful day.

We already have everything we need to be happy. We still tend to crave most what we can get the least. In other words, we want what we cannot have and we devalue what we do have, simply because we have it. If diamonds lay in piles by the Interstate, no one would be caught dead wearing them. But if there was only one diamond in the world, it would be priceless.

Happiness is not having what we want but wanting what we already have. When we define happiness in terms of what we want, we are always operating from a point of lack, discontent and negativity. We are focusing on what is missing from our lives, and we fool ourselves into thinking that something or someone else will fill that void and make us complete. But more of something or someone else does not bring fulfillment. When we want what we already have and express gratitude for it, we transform our lives into a positive experience. We see and feel the happiness that is all around us. When we are grateful for what we already have, we transform nothingness into abundance.

An Exercise Of Gratitude

Close your eyes and get comfortable. Take a deep breath and let your body relax. Inhale and exhale a few times. Think of as many things as you can that you're grateful for and that make your life worth living. Visualize what is precious in your life. See the things that you take for granted, things that if you didn't have them would leave your life empty. You can include both material items, such as your car or house, as well as relationships with loved ones, such as a child, spouse, lover or a pet. Let your thoughts come and visualize each one as vividly as you can. Acknowledge each important thought as it appears and feel the gratitude in your heart. Practice this exercise regularly so that you will begin to feel better about yourself and see how positive and rich your life already is.

Use the space below to record your thoughts and feelings about this exercise:

CHAPTER • 7

Life is in your hands. You can select joy if you want or you can find despair everywhere you look.

Leo Buscaglia

The Principle
Of Expectation

Our expectations have self-fulfilling effects that create our experiences and thus our experiences of life become whatever we expect them to be.

Murphy's Law says, "Whatever can go wrong will go wrong." This addictive way of thinking causes us to expect the worst life has to offer. We create self-defeating lives for ourselves, because negative thoughts haunt our minds:

- "If a tornado came through town, my house would be the very one it would strike."
- "There's no way I'll get chosen for that new job."
- "If we plan the party for outside, it will definitely rain."
- "Wouldn't you know it, I always get in the slowest grocery store line."
- "Bad luck follows me everywhere I go."
- "I'll be the last person on the supervisor's list to get a raise."

Murphy's Law is merely a negative way of thinking. The words we use reveal how the old negative thoughts dominate our lives through our actions. As we state them, we bestow on ourselves the very prophecy we would like to renounce. We carry impending doom with us everywhere and with thoughts like these, the worst usually does happen.

All of us have expectations. In our minds we create how events will unfold before they occur, and we enter situations with these mindsets. Usually when we expect a bad situation, it turns out that way because we unconsciously think and behave to make it fit with our expectations. We create positive situations in the same way . . . by thinking positive thoughts and behaving in ways that make them come true.

We discover in the healing process that the self-fulfilling prophecy is alive and well in our heads. When we think and expect the best, we usually reap positive results. Thinking the worst brings the worst into our lives. The Principle of Expectation says that our expectations influence our behaviors which, in turn, affect how others respond to us. A good illustration of how this principle works is "The Story of the Farmer and the Stranger."

The Farmer And The Stranger

Once there was a farmer working in the field, when down the road came a stranger.

"I've been thinking of moving," said the stranger, "And I wonder what kind of people live around here."

"Well," replied the farmer, "What kind of people live where you come from?"

"Not very good," answered the stranger. "They're selfish and mean and not at all friendly. I'll be glad to leave them behind!"

"Well," said the farmer, "I expect you'll find the same sort of people around here . . . selfish and mean and not at all friendly. You probably won't like it here."

The stranger went on.

Shortly afterwards, another stranger came along the same road.

"I've been thinking of moving," said the stranger, "and I wonder what kind of people live around here."

"Well," replied the farmer, "What kind of people live where you come from?"

"Oh, wonderful people!" answered the stranger. "They're generous and kind and very friendly. I'll really be sorry to leave them."

"Well," said the farmer, "I expect you'll find the same sort of people around here . . . generous and kind and very friendly. I'm sure you'll like it here."

The Power Of Expectations

On a cosmic level, metaphysics has long held that our thoughts and expectations create our realities of life. Joseph Murphy in his book, *The Cosmic Power Within You*, explains this process from a metaphysical viewpoint:

> Whatever your conscious reasoning mind accepts as true, engenders a corresponding reaction from your subconscious mind which is one with Infinite Intelligence within you. Your subconscious mind works through the creative law which responds to the nature of your thought, bringing about conditions, experiences and events in the image and likeness of your habitual thought patterns.

Scientists have known for a long time that our expectations affect the way we behave and that the way we behave affects how other people respond to us.

This basic principle has been demonstrated in the researcher's laboratory. Developmental psychologists conducted an experiment in which they asked a group of adults to rate the emotional behavior of a nine-month-old infant. One half of the adults were told that the infant was a boy and the other half were told they were observing a girl.

Results of the experiment showed that the same infant was thought to have different emotions, depending on whether the adults thought the infant was a boy or a girl. When presented with a jack-in-the-box, "girls" were thought to be *fearful* and "boys" were judged to be *angry*. Research has shown that these different expectations for boys and girls cause us to behave differently toward children based on their genders which, in turn, explains why girls develop such sex-stereotyped traits as dependency and boys develop traits such as aggression. Our expectations are fulfilled because of the way we treat children from birth. Many of these types of studies have been conducted in the scientist's laboratory and the conclusion is always the same.

Other studies have gone a step further with expectations and have shown consistently that whatever we expect, in fact, comes true for us.

The most famous experiment on self-fulfilling prophecies is called "Pygmalion in the Classroom." It dealt with the expectations that elementary school teachers had for their pupils' achievement. Teachers were told that a handful of their students had been identified as intellectual "late bloomers." Scores from a standardized test, the teachers were told, indicated these kids were expected to show unusually big achievement gains during the upcoming school year. The truth of the matter was that the children identified as exceptionally intelligent had, in fact, been randomly selected and placed in the classroom. So there was no reason, except for the teachers' mindsets, to expect high gains in achievement.

Achievement test results at the end of the school year showed that the children indeed did have higher leaps in performance. The gains were attributed to the self-fulfilling effects of teacher expectations. The researchers reasoned that the expectations teachers created about the special children caused them to treat the students differently, so that the children really did achieve more by the end of the year.

These studies and other mounting evidence indicate that any expectation can be fulfilling and that this process is not confined to the classroom.

Our expectations affect the way we behave, and the way we behave affects how other people respond to us.

Our strong beliefs or expectations about something have self-fulfilling prophecy effects, causing us to behave in ways that tend to make our expectations come true. When we break the "Pygmalion-in-the-Classroom" experiment down into small steps, it becomes clearer how the Principle of Expectation works:

1. The teacher expects specific behavior and achievement from particular students.
2. Because of these different expectations, the teacher behaves differently toward various students.
3. This treatment tells students what behavior and achievement the teacher expects from them and affects their self-concepts, achievement motivations and levels of aspiration.
4. If this treatment is consistent over time, and if students do not resist or change it in some way, it will shape their achievement and behavior. High-expectation students will be led to achieve at high levels, while the achievement of low-expectation students will decline.
5. With time, students' achievement and behavior will conform more and more closely to that originally expected of them.

Creating Outcomes

On a more practical everyday level, all of us create experiences based on what we expect to happen. A man reluctantly invited his mother for a visit. Although he loved her, he had difficulty being around her because she was so negative and grumpy. Two days before her visit he had butterflies in his stomach, thinking of the arguments that they would have and how upset she would make him. The man had already created the feelings and actions that would occur that weekend. Sure enough, all his negative images came true.

Everything that happens is a thought before it is an action. Artists create their masterpieces in their minds before putting them on canvas. The writer and musician have the thoughts of what they put on paper before they actively write the composition. We think about and practice what we'll say to the boss before asking for a raise. Thoughts about an event precede the actual event. When we have negative expectations about a situation, we're already creating the tone the action will take. Expecting problems, discontent and unhappiness brings us exactly that: problems, discontent and unhappiness. Imagining joy, abundance and happiness in one way or another will bring us these positive aspects of life. When we visualize positive consequences, we create positive situations.

Suppose, for example, you're going for a job interview. A friend tells you that the interviewer is friendly, kind and easy to talk to. No doubt you will go into the interview with an ease and calm that will be picked up by the employer, which will give him a positive impression of you. His positive impression, in turn, will indicate to you through his smiles and positive comments that he is impressed with you. This feedback will cause you to continue to present yourself in a self-enhancing way that will probably get you the job.

In contrast, suppose your friend tells you that the same man is a perfectionistic grouch. He is very hard to please, and you can never do anything right in his eyes. You will probably enter the job interview with apprehension. Your nervousness and uncertainty may cause you to forget to smile and to appear anxious and perhaps even incompetent. The employer senses your discomfort and forms an impression of you as edgy and unable to function under pressure. Your anxiety might even make him feel uncomfortable and cause him to develop a negative impression of you. You begin to feel his displeasure when he develops a cold, business-like demeanor in response to your seriousness and discomfort.

Fear Of Failure

Many of us are motivated from a fear of failure. At the very core of our fear is a deep feeling within that we are failures, no matter how successful we are in the outer world. We believe that we got where we are by luck or accident. It's only a matter of time until people will know the truth about us, that we are inadequate and unworthy.

When we carry the fear of failure, we expect to fail and unconsciously set ourselves up to do so. Our fear of failure becomes a self fulfilling prophecy, driving us so hard that we unintentionally sabotage our own success. It ruins our physical and emotional health. It cripples our relationships with co-workers, families and friends.

Emerson once said: *"You are what your thoughts make of you."* We become what we think about second to second and day to day.

Fear of failing is only a feeling that can be changed by our expectations. As we begin to think in new ways, we change our expectations. Once we believe what Franklin D. Roosevelt said about fear, "The only thing we have to fear is fear itself," we can change how we respond in many situations and thus eliminate any self-defeating habits that can lead to ultimate failure. We can willingly give up our fears of failing and rejection by accepting and loving ourselves unconditionally. In times when we fall short of our goals, we forgive ourselves and give ourselves credit for gains we did make. When we fail, we still see ourselves as winners because of our unyielding self-care and self-love.

Our mental outlook has a lot to do with how we live our lives. When we get upset by something that happens to us, it is not the situation that upsets us, but the way we think and feel about it. The event or action in our lives is not good, bad or fearful; it just *is*. The minute we judge it, based on our subjective thoughts, we are emotionally involved in it. Fearful thoughts bring fearful situations into our lives. We get stuck in a fearful way of life that is based on a past life of scary experiences. But when we think safe thoughts and expect nonthreatening events in our lives, we are filled with serenity and joy.

We can expect the best life has to offer. Looking for the good in ourselves and in others prepares us to reap the benefits of our positive thinking. Attuning to our spiritual selves fills us with positive energy that radiates throughout our bodies and into our relationships with others. We feel connected with people and serene in relationships.

Catastrophic Thinking

When the child let his guard down, the rapid-fire jolt of his father's drunken outbursts hit him like a jackhammer. So the boy learned to live with this uncertainty by always expecting the worst and staying poised for it, even when everything was okay. At least that way, even as an adult, he couldn't be caught off guard.

Sometimes the hardest part of the healing process is when everything is going well. "Things are just too good," we tell ourselves. "Something terrible is going to happen!" When there is quiet, it is the calm before the storm. When we spend the calm anticipating the storm, our lives are always stormy and full of thunder and lightning rather than peaceful. We are so accustomed to expecting only the worst, we do not know how to enjoy the best.

These negative expectations do not serve us anymore. They were born out of our turbulent past. Our past does not determine our future unless we let it. Our present mental attitudes determine what will happen next. When we are worried and anxious during *both* calm times *and* troubled times, then we create worried, fearful lives 24 hours a day.

Catastrophic thinking comes from thinking about the worst the future can bring. It is a continuation of addictive thinking from our dysfunctional past that we use to base our expectations for the future.

"What if a loved one dies?" "What if I don't get that job?" "What if it rains?" When we ask ourselves these questions, we worry about things we cannot control. "What ifs" are only thoughts that come from a past riddled with fear and depression. Many of the "what ifs" never happen, and we lose endless hours fretting for no reason when we could be enjoying the moment.

Asking ourselves "what if" questions is simply a way to generate needless anxiety and crisis in our lives. It is another form of addictive thinking that expects the worst, therefore creating the worst that can happen. "What ifs" make our lives unmanageable. As we heal, we accept the fact that "what ifs" are out of our control.

We can take "what is" and live in the present, for the now is all we have. Wayne Dyer said, *"Now is all we have. Everything that has ever happened to you and anything that is ever going to happen to you, is just a thought."*

How To Create What You Want

In his book, *You'll See It When You Believe It,* Wayne Dyer believes so strongly in this principle that he says we can create whatever we want in life simply by believing it first. We behave as if the desired event is in the process of happening and eventually we can make any dream come true. He does emphasize though that we must do more than wish. We must act in accordance with our desires and must be willing to do whatever it takes to make our desired outcomes materialize.

How To Create A Healthy Friendship

You can put your expectations to work for you rather than against you. Think of something you'd like to create in your life and follow the steps to have your desires manifested. Let's say, for example, you want to create a healthy friendship with someone.

1. First, get rid of any self-defeating thoughts that you are undeserving or unlikable or inadequate. You begin to think of yourself as worthy and likable based on your positive personality strengths. Visualize yourself meeting someone and interacting openly and genu-

inely with that person. The process requires that you truly believe that you are worthy and likable.

2. Behave in accordance with these expectations. You expect people to like you because you truly believe that you are worthy of their friendship. As a result of your beliefs and expectations, you behave differently as you come into contact with different people you meet. You have more confidence and enthusiasm. Perhaps you're more relaxed and more fun to be with.

3. All these traits impact on new people you meet in a positive way. Your self-confidence and self-appreciation attract others to you.

4. If you are persistent and consistent with your expectations about yourself over time, your positive actions will bring newcomers in your life and you will continue to draw people around you who are attracted to you.

5. Eventually you will find yourself in a new relationship with someone who likes you and enjoys your company as much as you enjoy theirs.

Just because we had a painful past doesn't mean we must continue living a painful life forever. We can create the type of life we want by changing how we look at the world. The 10 Principles of Healing teach us to change our expectations of the past and to look at the world differently.

As the story of the farmer and the stranger illustrates, we carry happiness or unhappiness with us everywhere we go. It is up to each of us to decide which we will expect. We can travel to the beaches of Maui or the jungles of the Amazon. But we will not find happiness there unless we take it with us. Many of us backpack our own problems and think our work, drugs or material comforts will make us happy. But the key to fulfillment is changing our thoughts and expectations through inner work.

The Expectation Experiment

This exercise is fun and quite revealing. It shows the power of the mind to manifest thoughts in our reality. It also demonstrates the power of our expectations and how they are transformed into our lives through the unconscious mind. You'll need a paper clip and six inches of sewing thread. Tie the string onto the top of either end of the paper clip. Hold the top of the string between your thumb and forefinger with the paper clip dangling on the other end.

Now close your eyes. Clear your mind of any distracting thoughts. Take a few deep breaths. Then imagine the paper clip moving in a clockwise circle. See it going in a circular motion in your mind's eye. Don't try to resist or force the string. Just concentrate on the image. After a few minutes, open your eyes and you'll see that the paper clip is behaving just exactly as you created it in your mind. Next close your eyes and imagine the paper clip moving counter clockwise. Then try visualizing it moving from side to side like a clock pendulum. Again you will see your mental image manifested in the real world as the paper clip swings from side to side. Finally, close your eyes and this time imagine the paper clip moving forward (away from your chest) and backwards (toward your chest). Again the paper clip behaves as you expected it to behave, as you imagined it in your mind.

This simple experiment demonstrates the power of suggestion and expectation and how we are influenced by our unconscious thoughts and expectations every minute we draw breath.

When we suggest to ourselves that we will fail, we will create failure. When we tell ourselves that it will be a rotten day, it will be. We can just as easily create positive outcomes by imaging them in our minds and telling ourselves that we are in store for good things to happen.

A Self-Fulfilling Visualization

Guided visualizations are helpful in learning to expect positive consequences and to create them in your life. Think of something you want to happen in your life. Sit in a comfortable position in a place where you will not be distracted for five or ten minutes. Close your eyes and focus on your breathing. Breathe in through the nose and out through the mouth several times. Let your body become completely relaxed. Continue breathing and relaxing until you are in a totally relaxed state.

See the desired outcome actually unfolding in your mind's eye. See yourself in situations where you expect the positive outcome to happen. See it happening vividly and image the smallest details of the event. Notice how you feel as it comes true. Notice how others around you feel.

After visualizing what you want several times in as many different ways as you can, open your eyes and state the desired outcome several times as if it is already taking place. Write it down two or three times and see it in print: *"I am now experiencing . . ."*

Repeat this exercise as often as you feel that it is necessary.

Everything is a thought before it is an actuality. The universe gives us life, but it is up to each of us to create our *experience* of that life. We create our lives through our thoughts. Whatever we believe to be true will be true for us. We see what we believe.

According to Shakti Gawain, in her book *Creative Visualization*,

"Simply having an idea or thought, holding it in your mind, is an energy which will tend to attract and create that form on the material plane. If you constantly think of illness, you eventually become ill; if you believe yourself to be beautiful, you become so."

Regardless of whether you take a metaphysical or a scientific point of view, the outcome can be the same when you think positive thoughts and have positive expectations of what you want.

What Do You Want?

You may imagine a satisfying job, a healthy relationship, a new house, inner serenity or greater prosperity. Name and visualize your desires as vividly as you can. See your expectations already coming true in your mind. Create these positive outcomes, visualize them often and don't let go of them. *Our thoughts can become actuality when we give them positive energy and experience them as if they are already coming true.* If the desired outcome doesn't occur, addictive thoughts could be standing in your way. Check to see what they are and how you can turn them around into positive expectations that will bring you a rewarding and fulfilling reality.

CHAPTER 8

The grass must bend when the wind blows over it.

Confucius

The Principle Of Harmony

Our lives work when we align our thoughts, feelings and actions to fit into the grand harmony of nature, rather than resist the natural forces of the universe.

On September 22, 1989, the eye of Hurricane Hugo struck my hometown of Charlotte, North Carolina. I was in Naples, Florida, giving a luncheon address to 1,000 people called, "Don't Worry; Be Happy." Needless to say, this was the ultimate test for me.

I spoke with my family by telephone as the wind ravaged our city. Naturally, I was concerned about my loved ones. But being hundreds of miles away, I knew I was powerless over the deadly winds of Hugo. The Serenity Prayer, the 12 Steps and the Principle of Harmony got me through the ordeal. Rather than fret about, "How can this be happening? Why is this happening to me? What if they are all killed?" I accepted the fact that "This *is* happening and I am powerless over the forces of a hurricane."

Knowing that there is a power greater than myself helped me turn the problem over to that power and to let go of the worry. The universe has functioned for millions of years without my worrying, controlling and forcing my self-will to help it. So things would surely work out this time without my input. I began fitting myself into the situation, rearranging my thoughts and feelings.

I repeated the Serenity Prayer: *"God grant me the serenity to accept the things I cannot change, courage to change the things I can and the wisdom to know the difference."* Obviously I could not change the course of hurricane winds. But I could change my thoughts, feelings and actions. Fitting into the scheme of what was happening actually empowered me and brought me serenity. I pulled the speech off without a hitch. I knew my family was resourceful enough to take care of themselves. I never worried another minute.

I had to stay an extra night in Florida because the Charlotte International Airport was closed due to runway damage. When I finally arrived home, I was stunned at the devastation of the city. We literally limped home from the airport through the cluttered streets. Electricity was out in over 90 percent of the city for two weeks and most residents had no water. Streetlights, electrical wires and huge trees lay across main thoroughfares. Cars lined up for gas for miles. Supermarkets were running out of food and because of a lack of refrigeration, perishables were unavailable. Ice became a valued commodity. Shoppers stood in endless lines and supermarkets only let a few people in the stores at a time. Schools were closed. There was no garbage collection. Television stations shut down. One-hundred-year-old oak trees blocked major intersections. It was impossible to drive in the city. A huge oak tree slammed into the roof of my car and my house suffered thousands of dollars worth of damage. Helicopters roared overhead. The entire city came to a standstill. It was an eerie sight.

So how does one respond to such total paralysis? This was a perfect time for me to employ the Principle of Harmony, for I was truly powerless. By accepting the disaster and taking action, rather than resisting or complaining, I made myself harmonious with it and surmounted the problem. I couldn't change what had happened, but I could change how I thought and acted in the situation. Like grass I was able to bend and flow, rather than resist and break. This is the Principle of Harmony.

Harmonious Living

Healing through the Principle of Harmony is nothing more than understanding and obeying the natural laws that govern the universe. We live on a planet that is perfectly planned. Our world is orderly and predictable because it is governed by laws that have operated from the beginning of time. The tides know how to move the oceans. Gravity knows how to hold things down. The planets know how to keep their alignment from the sun. The earth knows how to spin on its axis. Perfect harmony prevails.

Physicists agree that the universe operates in an orderly and explainable fashion rather than randomly and haphazardly. Scientists believe that the physical world unfolds according to the law of cause and effect. One event has the effect of causing another which causes another and so on.

Harmonious living requires that we learn to live our lives in accordance with the Principle of Harmony rather than push against the natural laws of nature. At birth we come into this perfectly-planned universe and try to change things around so that they fit with what we want. We unconsciously try to fit into the universal perfect circle our imperfect square pegs. We essentially try to change millions of years of perfect harmony. We throw a fit when it rains at an inconvenient time for us. We let the weather determine our moods rather than accepting it and going about our lives. We get frustrated in traffic jams. We become annoyed with people who have different beliefs and values from us. We get impatient in long slow-moving lines. We waste a lot of energy getting mad at our daily conditions, instead of accepting them and living our lives within their boundaries.

Disharmonious Living

Through disharmonious living, we create our own limitations that impoverish our lives and close ourselves off to healing experiences. Mindsets, routines, negative attitudes, fear of change, inflexibility, stinginess, impatience, anger, resentment, hesitation, withholding feelings and rigidity are all examples of disharmony. They clog our spiritual channels, preventing good from going out and from coming in. We create disharmony for ourselves in three ways:

1. **Forcing** is an *offensive* reaction to universal harmony in which we try to manipulate, control and impose our will on other people and situations.
2. **Resisting** is a *defensive* reaction to universal harmony in which we block the truth about other people or refuse to accept our life circumstances through denial or putting up resistance in some way.
3. **Clinging** is an *avoidance* reaction to the universal harmony in which we clutch the familiar and avoid change or the unknown in favor of habit and routine.

Are you a forcer, a resister or a clinger? Or are you all three?

Forcing: Stretching The Hours In A Day

Our need to put more hours in a day is an example of forcing our self-will. "There are just not enough hours in a day" is a constant refrain we often hear. It reflects our inability to accept things as they are and to live our lives within the universal framework. Stretching the day until it bulges at the seams and we're about to explode is an example of our trying to force the universe to fit our design, rather than our willingness to live within our human boundaries.

As the business world of machines and computers moves faster, we try to keep up with their frenzied pace. We hurry our kids to grow up, co-workers to rush against deadlines and life to move faster. Waiting lists and waiting rooms are not our cup of tea. We want the cashier to move the lines through quicker and the physician to see us immediately upon our arrival.

But we are not automotive machines; we are human beings. We were not made to accelerate at 90 miles an hour, day in and day out. When we push our engines too far and too fast, we burn out. Stress and physical side effects appear and we shut down.

We can ask ourselves what we are racing from. Do we overload ourselves with commitments to feel worthy? Does our quick-step lifestyle keep us from facing a storehouse of hurtful feelings? Or do we keep busy perhaps to escape from intimacy, from fears of rejection and abandonment, or from feelings of low self-worth that are too painful to confront? The Principle of Harmony brings us new and different ways of thinking about our actions. It puts back the harmony and meaning in being alive. The rat race is won when we begin our healing journey with just one pace.

There are 24 hours in a day because the universe was designed that way. Our lives start working as we structure our days for only 24 hours and not 40. Going with, rather than forcing the rhythm and pulse of the universe, we are less stressed, just as productive, and have time for personal reflection in each day. We can sigh with relief when we deflate our days with less doing and lighten them with more being.

Henry Miller said, "The world is *not* to be put in order, the world *is* order incarnate. It is for us to put ourselves in unison with this order." Freedom comes from knowing what our options are. Some things cannot be changed no matter what. No matter how hard we try, we cannot make our world and the people in it behave as we want. The universe is not at our beck and call and does not operate according to our whims. It functions from a higher knowing that is independent from us.

We can want our spouse or lover to have dinner on the table, keep the kids "out of our hair" or pay the bills on time. We can want our loved ones to live their lives to suit us. We can want our boss to give us a promotion, to like us or to give us a raise. We can want the tree outside our window to fly, too, but all the forcing, wishing, manipulating and griping in the world will never make these things happen.

Sometimes we feel that our lives are a battleground. Life can be one perpetual struggle after another, one battle after another. We cannot persuade the boss to see our point of view; we cannot scrounge enough money to purchase the new car; we cannot sway the opinions of colleagues to reach a decision at work; we cannot convince our lover, spouse or roommate that our decision about the household makes the most sense.

We may find ourselves constantly arguing with family members or harshly disagreeing with co-workers. Everybody in our life, it seems, is against us. After a while we must face the facts. We cannot always be right and everyone else always wrong. If we are constantly squabbling with others, what are we doing to create the tension? Even when we know in our hearts that our idea stinks, that our actions are wrong or that a colleague has thought of a better way, our stubborn ego refuses to concede.

When we feel as if we are constantly battling and losing, we can step back and look at what's going on. Sometimes we unconsciously draw battle lines with our combative attitudes. We try to force our will by refusing to hear other points of view. We keep alert and prepared to strike with combative approaches that others feel are argumentative, aggressive, overbearing, arrogant, and self-indulgent. We create war within ourselves without even knowing it.

It is not our responsibility to put the world in perfect order as we believe it *should* be. The world is perfectly ordered as it is. Life is not tailored to our specifications, and it does not bend to fit our lifestyles. The universe has operated by its own laws since the beginning of time and doesn't change for any of us. Still, we try to make our lives work as we want them to by our rules. We use a lot of energy trying to fit a size nine foot into a size six shoe, riding horses in the opposite direction from which they are headed and trying to make trees fly.

Forcing comes from fear of not being able to control. The solution is to admit our powerlessness and to let go of the need to control. We can stop trying so hard, let things be and put ourselves in unison with the universal flow. We cannot change our spouses or parents to be the kind of people we want them to be, no matter how hard we try. We can only accept them as they are and change our reactions to them. Freedom and serenity come from accepting things as they are, living our lives within these boundaries. We accept ourselves, not partially, but as a total package with strong and weak qualities and lavish love on ourselves despite human limitations. We accept things in our lives that we cannot control or change, and we change the old negative thoughts and emotions to more optimistic ways of thinking, feeling and being.

As long as we try to tell the stars how to shine and the sun how to set, we experience frustration and failure. As long as we think we know how to conduct our lives without guidance from a higher self, we will make a mess of things. But once we learn the universal rules, we fit into the grand harmony. Peace, happiness and serenity are ours. Healing is an ongoing process of learning what the universal principles are and how we can align with them rather than resist them. This is what 12-Step work is all about: accepting the fact that we are powerless over the way the world functions. The planets and stars do not align based on how we want them to and the tides will not change for our whims. We have no choice but to align our thoughts, feelings and behaviors to the universal flow. Healing is a relearning process in which we discover how to live our lives in harmony with the natural flow of the universe. In recovery we move in the direction the river is going rather than pushing against it. Our first step in this transformation is to change our thinking and perception of ourselves and the world around us.

Resisting: Unwilling To Bend

Tropical palms are very sturdy trees. They survive, not because they stand rigid and hard against tropical storms, but because they are flexible enough to bend, swing and sway with the force of the wind. Few of us have the fluidity of these wondrous trees because we live straitjacketed lives. Our lives are like clockwork. We have a daily routine that we follow to the letter. We dot every *i* and cross every *t*. We never divert from our schedules and never make exceptions to the rules. We call this being efficient.

Have we straitjacketed ourselves into a lifestyle that doesn't know spontaneity or flexibility? Who says we cannot take a walk through the park with a friend on our lunch hour? Who says we can't decide after work to go out to eat on the spur of the moment? Who says we cannot walk barefoot in a summer rainstorm without an umbrella? We put our own limitations on our lives. We can loosen ourselves by becoming flexible, spontaneous and willing to bend.

Resistance in our daily lives stalls the healing process and brings it to a standstill. When we put up resistance, we insulate ourselves from universal harmony. We block the natural flow. We survive life more easily when we can bend with life's burdens like the tropical palms against the wind. If we're rigid and stiff and resist, we break. Sometimes our stiffness and resistance cause us to over-react to the little things in life. The light bulb burns out in the bathroom while we are getting ready for work. The car has a flat tire on the way to the market. The television is on the blink. "The house is falling apart!" we scream. We slam doors and rant and rave.

When small problems add up, they can fill a volume and we act as if the world will end. Our tantrums in reaction to life's small events reflect our inability to accept the way the world operates. It is a simple fact of life that worldly things break down, disintegrate and wear out. When we find ourselves over-reacting to little things, we can put minor annoyances in proper perspective and realize that things are not as bad as they seem.

The house isn't really coming unglued just because an appliance breaks or a gadget wears out. Once we see how trivial little things are in the grand scheme of life, we act rather than react. We accept them as a small part of life, they fail to dominate our emotions and we go about our day.

There is a difference between stubbornness and persistence. We are persistent when we know we are right and when blocked, we look for new ways to achieve our purpose. We are stubborn when we know we are wrong and cannot admit it or when we insist on one closed avenue rather than exploring others that are open to us. Always being right keeps us stuck in unhappiness and defies the Principle of Harmony which teaches us acceptance over self-will.

Stubbornness is another expression of self-will to have things as we want them to be, an unwillingness to accept things as they are. When we stubbornly refuse to give in, we resist the truth. Nothing goes out and nothing comes in. As we let go and let God, our spiritual channels are cleared of stubborn resistance.

Clinging: Unable To Let Go

A big part of being willing to bend is being fluid, spontaneous and flexible and accepting change in our lives. Everything in nature is constantly changing. The seasons change; the earth is constantly moving; the planets are rotating; people are born, die and move out of town. Human beings are the most adaptable of all living creatures, yet we resist change. Whether the change is sought or imposed or happens by chance or design, the typical response is to cling to old habits which straitjacket us. It keeps us stuck in the past and gives us a distorted image of today's reality. We form narrow inaccurate ideas about ourselves and others based on old information that no longer applies in the present.

Change is one of the few things in life we can count on and no matter how hard we clutch the past, change will drag us kicking and screaming into the present. Edmund Burke once said, *"We must all obey the great law of change. It is the most powerful law of nature."* Change is inevitable and when we cling to the familiar and the comfortable, we avoid change.

Another way of bending is to deliberately eliminate sameness and institute change in our lives by opening ourselves to new experiences.

A white-water rafting enthusiast was bored with the small rapids of a river where she regularly boated. A friend advised her of another river with faster and higher currents. But she balked, saying she was afraid to give the new rapids a try and went back to the river she had already mastered.

We don't get very far going back to the same spot all the time. Although it may feel comfortable, even secure, healing comes from moving forward, not moving backward or standing still. Faced with fear, how many of us turn and walk away? Safety precautions aside, we heal when we walk into and face our fears. When we walk the other way, fear wins the battle and continues to dominate us. Once we face it, we conquer it.

Is there something you're afraid to say to a colleague? Do you want to admit something to a friend? Is there something within you that you are afraid to face? You can ask yourself, "What fears are standing in the way of my progress and what can I do to walk through them?"

Do we embrace the adventures and changes in our lives? Or do we retreat from them? Being healed means mending our ways, changing addictive thoughts, feelings and behaviors so that they fit our new lives.

The healing process is underway as we change old habits. We give up forcing, resisting and clinging in our lives, and take more responsibility for our personal healing.

Change, discomfort and the unknown become bridges to a new way of being. Once we stop resisting our life flow, we feel the healing taking place, and we can see the consequences as they unfold in our daily lives. We still have problems and concerns, but we approach them in more optimistic and effective ways.

Taoism

Western culture was founded on the belief that nature is to be challenged, fought, and conquered. Our forefathers, for example, sought to tame the wild west in this country. We have a history of disharmony with nature that has been passed down to us today. Ecologically, we still plod ahead with our human goals and desires, regardless of how they fit in with the synchronism of the environment, much less our harmony with it. Because of our disharmony, we are in trouble with our toxic waste, as well as our toxic thinking and toxic relationships. The Principle of Harmony is sometimes hard for North Americans to accept and understand because of our disharmonious legacy.

Eastern culture, on the other hand, is based on living in harmony with nature and yielding to its forces. According to the ancient Taoist (pronounced DOWIST) philosophy, our purpose in life is to learn valuable lessons from life's experiences. Life's lessons need to be learned, just as its laws need to be followed, to create harmony. The problem is that most of us don't know what these laws are so we live our lives aimlessly, hoping we will somehow stumble upon happiness and miraculously discover the person of our dreams.

The Tao is the mysterious entity that resides within our innermost being and works throughout the cosmic universe.

Many great beliefs and religions, as well as the 12 Steps and Taoism, believe in *going with the flow of a Higher Power*, rather than trying to force our own will. Several other principles such as "Be here now," "Let go and let God" and "Keep it simple" also are common threads found throughout these different beliefs.

Put into its simplest form, Taoism is harmonious living. It means putting into practice our appreciation and learning from whatever happens to us in our daily lives. Rather than resisting or fleeing from life's circumstances, we face them and find meaning and purpose and learn from them, no matter how painful or fearful they may be. It involves quieting ourselves through meditation or prayer so that we connect with the universal energy that tells us what we need to know or do in our lives. The natural outcome of moving in harmony with this universal flow, rather than manipulating or controlling it, is profound contentment and happiness.

How can we expect to have harmonious relationships and lives that work when we are out of harmony with ourselves? We search for serenity and happiness. We want to lead healthy, fulfilling lives. Yet we continue to encounter anxiety, problems, disharmonious relationships, fear and sadness. Why? Because addictive thinking keeps us out of harmony with ourselves.

Like our cowboy ancestors, we have tried to make our lives work by changing the outside world and we've looked in the wrong place for the key as the tale of Nasrudin suggests. Our lives begin to work and we start to achieve our desired lives once we work from the inside out, rather than the outside in.

Connecting with our inner selves can turn all this around. We let go of trying to manipulate and control our lives. We stop trying to force things to happen that are beyond our control. We stop trying so hard. We let the world — everyone in it, ourselves included — be. We stop pushing against the current of the river because we learn that it flows by itself, and we learn to flow with it and live in the present. We discover that when we let go of circumstances, they work out better than when we interfere with them. We move from human *doing* to human *being*.

As we let ourselves be, we start to become fulfilled one day at a time. As the philosopher Lao Tzu said, "*The way to do is to be.*"

Simplicity

"Keep it simple" is a term we hear a lot on our healing path. Simplicity is the cornerstone of spiritual development. The message is simple: one step at a time and one day at a time. The goal is simple: knowing and being ourselves. The tools are simple: step by step and easy does it. Daily meditations and the 12 Steps are other tools that can be used.

Our lives become jumbled with acquiring material possessions and achieving outward success and importance. The more we try to analyze and rationalize our lives, the more complicated and crowded our thoughts become. We take our problems and obsess and worry. We turn them over and over in our minds and examine them from every angle. They grow bigger and bigger and become more complicated than they actually are.

Taoism says that things in their original simplicity contain their own natural power, power that is spoiled or lost when that simplicity is changed. Clutter and complications of the material world can interfere with our healing path. A simple approach to our personal search cuts through the complications of our everyday lives. Answers are always there. Using the simple tools that we are given keeps our path clear of clutter.

Meditations For Living In Harmony

Surrendering to resistance allows us to go with the flow and, rather than pushing against the current, to ride the river in the direction that it takes us. Releasing ourselves from resistance unclogs our spiritual channel, bringing open-mindedness, positive attitudes, adventure, flexibility, patience, generosity, forgiveness, love, fluidity and spontaneity. Letting go of resistance and accepting the unknown takes us to other ways of being . . . a change that need not be threatening when we have faith in a power greater than ourselves. When we let go and let God, our lives flow with ease.

In your daily life when you find yourself forcing situations into coming true, resisting situations over which you have no control or clinging to things or people, step back from the situation. Look objectively at what's going on. Ask yourself why you're forcing, resisting or clinging. Ask why your self-will is overpowering you. Let it go. Obviously the universe has something else in store for you. Look at other courses of action that are less complicated and that unfold with more ease.

The following affirmations can help you let go and live more harmoniously. Memorize them and say them silently to yourself when you are having difficulty with giving up control.

FORCING: I admit that I am powerless over controlling my world and that when I force things, my life becomes unmanageable. A Power greater than myself can restore me to sanity. I turn my will and my life over to the care of this Higher Power.

RESISTING: Today I do not allow resistance to stunt my growth. I will catch myself when I start to resist against what life doles out. I will give up the resistance and open myself to the lessons that life teaches me. I do not fear the unknown because the universal power controls it.

CLINGING: Today I practice hands off and follow the grand harmony of the universal forces. Rather than clinging to old ways and familiar habits, I am open to change. I am learning the rules of life and how fitting into them can foster my healing and growth.

SERENITY: God, grant me the serenity to accept the things I cannot change, the courage to change the things I can and the wisdom to know the difference.

Are you a forcer, a resister or a clinger? Think of as many things as you can that you have been forcing, resisting or clinging to in your own life. It can be resistance to a life change, refusal to accept someone's behavior or unwillingness to try something new. Below list each aspect of your life that you are forcing, resisting or clinging to in one column. Beside it put what you can do to let go of and accept this part of your life over which you have no control.

Forcing   **Acceptance**

Resisting   **Acceptance**

Clinging   **Acceptance**

Letting-Go Exercise

Now close your eyes and visualize letting go of all the things that you have forced, resisted or clung to, opening yourself up to the natural order of life. Visualize your powerlessness. See yourself giving up trying to change or control things any longer. See yourself flowing with your life which is in harmony with the universal plan.

This exercise will lift heavy burdens and bring relief when you realize you no longer have to bear them.

Experience your renewed feelings of serenity and harmony as you begin to let go.

Write your thoughts and feelings in the space below.

CHAPTER 9

No one can make you feel inferior without your consent.

Eleanor Roosevelt

The Principle
Of Empowerment

We are empowered when we think of ourselves as survivors instead of victims of life and when we accept responsibility for our thoughts, feelings and actions.

Harriet lay in her hospital bed complaining of how sick she was. "There's nothing I can do," she moaned. "My husband has worried me so with his drinking. That's what put me here. He doesn't care about me and treats me like a dog. He's never home and when he is, he never pays me any attention. He's got me so far down that I can't help myself anymore. He's made me think that I'm nothing. If it weren't for him, I wouldn't be in such a bad fix. It's his fault that I had to check into the hospital in the first place!"

Are You An Externalizer Or An Internalizer?

Harriet's addictive thoughts keep her stuck in the role of helpless victim that she learned in childhood. Studies indicate that this type of addictive thinking is bred in dysfunctional homes. Control is a big issue for children from dysfunctional families because they have witnessed one or both parents struggling, without much success, to maintain control and manage their own lives. Paralyzed from the stresses and strains of a dysfunctional upbringing, often children are unable to develop an effective ability to manage their lives. Adults who grew up in dysfunctional families are more likely than adults from more stable backgrounds to become what psychologists call *externalizers*. Simply put, this means they think of themselves as helpless pawns of fate whose lives are determined by external forces outside of themselves. As a result, they externalize their responsibilities, resign themselves to their circumstances and succumb to the guides of fate and chance. They feel little or no responsibility for what happens to them and blame other people and situations for their problems. Externalizers believe that they are blamed for things that are not their fault, that it doesn't pay to try hard because things never turn out right anyway and that people are mean to them for no reason at all.

This body of research suggests that when we grow up in dysfunctional homes, we develop "learned helplessness" — that no matter what we do, our fate is out of our hands. We are at greater risk of being victimized by life rather than empowered by it. But the good news is that by changing their addictive thinking, *externalizers* can become *internalizers*.

Internalizers believe that control of their lives comes from inside themselves. They are masters of their own fate and bear personal responsibility for what happens to them. They believe their own actions determine the positive or negative outcomes in their lives. Internalizers believe that if they do something wrong, they can do something to make it right, that they can change what might happen tomorrow by what they do today. Research indicates that those who perceive themselves as being "at cause" instead of "at effect" in their own lives tend to be more optimistic and respond more positively in general to the circumstances they encounter. Externalized thinking can be changed to internalized thinking through the Principle of Empowerment.

The Principle of Empowerment says that it is not what life deals us that determines our happiness or unhappiness. It is how we think and act to what life deals us that makes the difference. The universe gives us life, but we have the power to create our experience of life. If we think of ourselves as helpless victims at the mercy of life's blows, then we will be truly miserable. If we view ourselves as empowered to use life's disadvantages to learn and improve our own lives, then we create a positive experience out of a negative one.

The ways in which we think about what happens to us create our emotions and reactions, not the incidents themselves. When we think of ourselves as victims of life, we automatically imprison ourselves. Staying focused on hardships and problems keeps us stuck in addictive thinking (pessimism, loss of choice, past negative perceptions, catastrophic thinking). We believe that we are made miserable by the circumstances of life. We become attached to thinking of ourselves as downtrodden. Failure, despair and pessimism become a chronic way of life. Essentially we become addicted to self-victimization and self-pity. We use them to blame others for our plight and get us off the responsibility hook.

Blaming Others

An addictive-thinking woman went to her boss and complained that the new employee with whom she shared an office "made her nervous" because she talked too much. The complaining woman asked the boss to move the officemate somewhere else, which he promptly did. Two weeks later the complaining woman moaned that her second officemate "made her mad" because she was so messy. Again the boss accommodated her request to move the messy newcomer. Clearly the problem belonged to the complaining woman. She blamed others for her own feelings, refusing to deal with her problems in a mature way and depending upon others to solve her difficulties for her. Her boss, who was more than willing to accommodate, simply enabled the woman's addictive thinking and unknowingly stunted her growth.

Below are some of the famous last words from addicted thinkers who perceive themselves as victims:

- "You ruined my life!"
- "He makes me so mad."
- "I would have done a better job if you hadn't bothered me."
- "You're driving me crazy."
- "People are always putting me down."
- "She treats me so mean."
- "I wouldn't drink if you wouldn't nag so much."
- "You hurried me and caused me to make a mistake."
- "It's not my fault."
- "I can't help it."
- "They forced me to use bad language by the way they talked to me."
- "Most people don't like me."
- "My life is over because of the way they treated me."
- "I was doing fine until you interrupted me."
- "I'm a compulsive overeater because of the way my parents treated me."
- "It's just the way I am."
- "I never get any food because I always have to be the last one in line."
- "I wouldn't be in this fix if it weren't for you!"
- "If you would just change your ways, everything would be okay."
- "My high-pressured job is making me a workaholic."
- "Look what you've done to me now!"

Nobody *makes* us sick, angry, nervous or anything else unless we let them. These famous last words are ways of shirking responsibilities for our feelings and making ourselves victims of life rather than survivors of it. Our thoughts and emotions are *our* own making. No one makes them for us. Addictive thinking leads us to believe that our problems and solutions are outside of us. So we blame other people for our downfalls and feel self-pity. We say it's the circumstance in which we find ourselves that causes our pain and suffering. It's the way other people treat us or it's because of a bad break. We waste a lot of time and energy berating others. As long as we blame other people or situations for our problems, we never get to the reason for the state that we're in. Putting the blame on someone else prevents us from accepting the responsibility for changing our lives for the better and happiness eludes us.

Believing that our problems and solutions are outside of us causes us to think that we have no say-so over our lives and that everything that happens to us is determined by fate, chance and other people, events and situations. We blame fast-track corporate America for the widespread workaholism. We blame nagging spouses for our alcoholism. We blame our parents for addictive relationships and so on.

Regardless of what happened or is happening to us, it is our responsibility to change it. Nobody else can do that for us. Recovery teaches us that it isn't the world or the people in it who make us unhappy. It's the way we think about the people and the world that makes us unhappy.

Facing problems and owning them when they are truly ours help us become responsible for our thoughts, feelings and actions. Being responsible for our feelings, rather than blaming others, puts us further down the road of healing. The thoughts and feelings that we harbor inside are responsible for everything that happens to us. As long as we blame the outside world for our lot, we remain victims and disempower ourselves. Once we accept responsibility for our thoughts, feelings and actions, we empower ourselves and our lives improve. What in our own lives do we need to take responsibility for that we have been blaming on someone else?

We also victimize ourselves when we take the blame for the actions of others. Self-empowerment helps us stop feeling the emotions that belong to someone else and to feel our own emotions. We stop being responsible for others and become responsible for ourselves. We start feeling that we count for something and start standing up for ourselves. We stop blaming and whining about our circumstances, and take proper actions to change them.

Helplessness And Powerlessness

All of us are powerless, but none of us are helpless. Admitting our powerlessness is the first fundamental step in the 12 Steps that begins our spiritual awakening. Recovery teaches us that lust for power is a mirage in a spiritually barren desert. We discover that no matter how hard we try, we can never attain the power to control our lives or anyone else's. We are powerless by ourselves, and our quest for power has made our lives unmanageable. Relinquishing our power to a spiritual source paradoxically empowers us and makes us survivors of life.

Powerlessness does not mean that we are helpless. Helplessness is simply an addictive way of thinking that enables self-victimization. Helpless thoughts are addictive thoughts that impede our spiritual journey.

We are powerless over the actions of family, friends, colleagues, tides and the weather. But we are empowered through our own thoughts and actions. We are powerless over the weather, but we are not helpless when it comes to our attitudes toward rain and snow. Helplessness occurs when we do not exercise the courage to change the things in our lives that we can.

We are powerless over the external world, but we have inner power to heal ourselves by choosing how we think, feel and behave. Powerlessness does not mean throwing the control of our lives out of the window. We do not give our personal power to gurus, therapists, spouses, writers or lovers to exercise control over us. Relinquishing our personal power to another human being makes us helpless co-dependent victims of life. Serenity comes from accepting our powerlessness over those things we cannot change, courage to change the things we can and wisdom to know the difference.

From Victim To Victory

It takes a resourceful mind to make a feast when the cupboard is bare. It's ingenious to take junk and turn it into useful treasures. It is a challenge to transform daily experiences into useful rather than damaging consequences. There is always a silver lining in each cloud, positive in the negative, good in the bad. We make something out of nothing by turning situations around to our advantage. Using every experience, no matter how painful or difficult, as lessons from which to grow is a no-lose, no-victim situation. It empowers us with the ability to always survive and to live our lives with dignity and quality.

The best example in my own life is again Hurricane Hugo. Accepting our powerlessness over the circumstances paradoxically empowered us to free ourselves from the devastation and to take action. The city of Charlotte responded with wonderful spirit. Everyone was a trooper. Neighbor helped neighbor by removing tree limbs, clearing debris or covering broken car windows with plastic. Some people used their chain saws to cut up trees. Others cooked food and made drinks. Everybody seemed to be empowered by the experience. In my neighborhood no one sat and whined about their losses . . . which were considerable. There were no victims of Hugo, just survivors. A block party was held and thawed food was thrown on grills that were stationed at various points in the street. For two weeks our families ate by candlelight whatever was on hand for evening meals. We didn't have television and we talked and communicated. We went to bed early and got lots of needed rest. Despite its devastation, Hurricane Hugo enriched the lives of many people by giving them a deeper appreciation of each other and their lives in general.

Self-empowerment comes from choosing how we interpret situations. We have the power to choose how we will interpret the past as well as how we will live our lives in the future. Admitting we are powerless over what *was* paradoxically gives us power to respond to what *will be*. Once we recognize that we have power to create our thoughts, we stop making ourselves victims of circumstances.

I spent most of my life believing I was a victim of a dysfunctional family. These addictive thoughts were bars on a cage in which I had mentally imprisoned myself. My mental prison kept me disempowered and I had no say-so over my life. As an adult, my cycle of misery continued just as if my alcoholic father (who had died five years before) were still in control of my fate.

One of the most important things I learned in recovery was to think empowering thoughts. As I began to liberate my addictive thinking, I no longer saw myself as a disempowered victim of unfortunate circumstances. I learned to give up those feelings of victimization and to see myself as a person of worth and power. My whole life began to change. Using my childhood background as a transformational experience from which to learn, I began to reinterpret my life in a more positive and constructive way. Everything that had happened to me as a child of an alcoholic had happened for reasons, both good and bad. Those difficult times led me to where I am right now: writing books and lecturing around the country on the addictive process. That is a fulfilling thought.

An empowered person is learning life's lessons, whereas a victim is enduring life's pain. Empowerment means taking conscious responsibility for your life, instead of blaming others for your problems. Your life does not have to be bleak and traumatic.

You can choose to view yourself as a victim of an addictive past and continue living in misery. Or you can declare yourself a survivor and use your painful experiences as lessons that teach you to live with quality.

A Vietnam veteran who lost an arm uses the empathy and compassion he learned to counsel disabled survivors of war. A person with AIDS volunteers time to help raise money for AIDS research. A woman, sexually abused in childhood, writes a book about her recovery to help other incest survivors.

Author Bernie Siegel told of a seven-year-old boy whose own words reflected how he saw himself as a *survivor* of cancer instead of a victim of the disease: "If God wanted me to be a basketball player, he'd made me seven feet tall. Instead, he gave me cancer so I can be a doctor and help other people."

This child turned his cancer into an act of love. It empowered him over his disease, and shows us that no matter how horrendous our yesterdays, we can transform them into meaningful and fulfilling todays and tomorrows. Everybody experiences emotional pain and suffering. The important thing is what we do with it. Turning obstacles into opportunities empowers us with dignity and grace.

Empowering Yourself Through Thought Reconstruction

The technique of thought reconstruction puts problems into a more positive and workable light. It allows us to approach our hardships from an angle of survivorship in which we can do something about them. Thought reconstruction allows us to change the labels we hang on events so that the new tags generate more positive emotions.

Many people with AIDS, for example, discover that the disease brings suffering and worry but that it also gives an opportunity to learn, give and grow. They favor the empowering terms of "AIDS survivor" or "person with AIDS," instead of disempowering names such as "AIDS victim." "AIDS victims" are helpless and are to be pitied. "AIDS survivors" are in charge of their lives and live more fully by managing their lives to the maximum despite their conditions, rather than focusing on their helplessness. Survivors live their lives with dignity and demand respect and admiration rather than pity.

The thought reconstruction process allows us to assemble all the thinking skills from the other 10 Principles of Healing to overcome life's difficulties. We direct our gaze away from hardships and look for the possibilities.

We focus on healthier perceptions, optimism, choice and positive expectations. As we practice these earlier principles, we automatically empower ourselves. Instead of perceiving ourselves as victims and hence powerless, we change our addictive thinking in a positive direction to live our lives to the fullest.

Empowerment comes when we are down and out and all hope seems to be gone, yet we know it is not the world but our own mental attitude that needs changing. Knowing that we cannot change the world, but that we can change our view of it, allows us to change our whole existence from helplessness to empowerment.

Achieving happiness and serenity does not depend on anyone but us. Thought reconstruction helps us survive troubles rather than being victimized by them. It is up to each and every one of us to face ourselves truthfully by taking charge of our lives. No one imprisions us but ourselves, and we build the bars high, wide and thick. Many of us victimize ourselves through our own self-limitations that prevent us from living fully. Empowerment is about reframing our addictive-thinking mirrors. We look back and examine the people who mirrored those destructive images to us, and we see that things were not that way at all. We look into a new looking-glass self that reflects joy, beauty and truth. We become a shining mirror for others to help them see their own human magnificence.

Thought Reconstruction Exercise

The Situation: Think of a time in which you felt helpless or victimized. Objectively describe the situation in the blanks without including your thoughts and feelings about the situation. _____

_____

_____

Your Addictive Reactions: Describe your helpless and victimized thoughts, feelings and actions in the blanks without self-blaming or self-shaming. _____

_____

_____

Thought Reconstruction: Reconstruct your addictive reactions in a way that they empower you and give you some say-so over your helpless thoughts and feelings and enable you to reassess the situation as an opportunity instead of an obstacle. _____

_____

_____

You can use the thought reconstruction technique any time you catch yourself in self-victimization thinking. This exercise can help you overcome helpless thoughts, feelings and actions and surmount obstacles in your life.

Reclaiming The Power In Your Life

Life is chock full of joy. Still, we might say, "There's no joy in *my* life. It's full of nothing but heartache and despair." We victimize ourselves with our pain and suffering through these addictive thoughts. We allow our thoughts to be determined by those with whom we live, work and play. We become so accustomed to grabbing onto their pain and hurt that we miss riding our own wave of joy.

It is comforting to know that just because others cannot feel joy in their hearts doesn't mean it's not there for us. We can create it. Regardless of what happens in the hustle and bustle of daily life, we can empower ourselves to radiate joy. We don't have to wait for someone else to be joyful before we allow ourselves to express it. We don't have to have a reason to be joyful. We can simply choose it, regardless of the moods of those around us. Joy is around and within us. All we have to do is connect with it. No matter how low our material world falls, we can keep our spiritual selves up by reviving the joy in our lives.

Sometimes we want to feel joy but we truly feel anguish. We want to explode with enthusiasm but our emptiness keeps us from mustering it. Our mind chooses love but our heart is not in it. We want to be generous but possessiveness holds us back.

Where do we start when the spirit and mind are not in harmony? Thought reconstruction.

Thinking "as if" we are the way we want to be eventually changes our attitudes and feelings until we are the way we want to be. We can begin thinking and acting "as if" we are happy by smiling and complimenting someone else. Or we can act with enthusiasm until we start to feel it inside. We can think "as if" we are confident when we give a speech, even though our heart flutters and we tremble inside.

Sometimes it is necessary to start with empowering thoughts to get our emotions and behaviors to follow suit. Thinking "as if" jump starts our heart and turns blue moods and sour attitudes into more positive mental outlooks. No matter what the moods of those around us or the tone of the situation, we can create how we want to be by thinking and acting "as if." Eventually our "as if" and "as is" thoughts, feelings and actions will align.

Taking action and making conscious decisions for ourselves are also a big part of being responsible for reclaiming the power in our lives. When we feel indecisive, we can take action. Any action is better than none. When we leave decisions up to other people and situations, we lose our power and victimize ourselves. Making conscious choices puts us in the position of being survivors of life. Never again can we rely on such excuses as "It's not my fault" or "I can't help it." What action can you take in your own life to empower yourself that you have left up to another person or a chance situation?

There are some things about our lives over which we can exercise choice and others over which we cannot. Once we see where our options and possibilities lie, we can make more conscious decisions and gain freedom and empowerment.

Empowering Yourself

The following exercise can help you reclaim the power in your life by taking action on matters you have left to chance. In the first column name a hardship in your life; in the second column describe what you have to accept about the situation; and in the third column identify aspects about the situation that you can choose. I have given you two examples to get you going.

The Problem	I Can Accept	I Can Choose
1. My spouse ran away with someone else.	The relationship is over.	I can forgive them and know that there's nothing wrong with me.
2. My friend is a negative person.	I cannot change my friend's negativity.	I can be a positive person, regardless of how others think.
_____	_____	_____
_____	_____	_____
_____	_____	_____
_____	_____	_____
_____	_____	_____
_____	_____	_____
_____	_____	_____
_____	_____	_____

CHAPTER 10

When you shake your fist at someone, remember that all your fingers are pointing at yourself.

Jacob Braude

The Principle
Of The Boomerang

The thoughts we put out from within eventually come back to us in one form or another . . . just like a boomerang.

Sending out positive thoughts, feelings and actions causes positive experiences to come back to us. But if we think ugly hateful thoughts, then ugly hateful things happen to us, perhaps not right away, but they manifest in our lives eventually. The Boomerang Principle holds that changing negative destructive thoughts, words and actions into constructive ones yields positive life experiences.

One Is A Whole Number

Metaphysics holds that we are all one vast energy source. We are all interconnected, as is everything in the universe. No matter how much we want to be separate and individual, we're linked to the whole. We are all one great mass of subatomic particles each with our own electromagnetic energy field. The concept of oneness has credibility in scientific circles. Physicists claim that when atoms within a molecule align in a certain way and a critical mass number is reached, the rest of the atoms spontaneously line up the same way. When enough people agree on what is real, once a critical mass is reached, everyone will see reality similarly. As the critical mass of a species thinks and acts in a certain way, the remainder of the species will follow suit. Psychologist Carl Jung spoke of the "Collective Unconscious" that links each of us with the rest of the people in the world, influencing one another in subconscious ways.

Taoism speaks of the *yin* and *yang*, the extremes in life — good and bad, love and hate, joy and sadness, masculine and feminine — that represent the interconnectedness, harmony and transformation of everything.

The yin and yang of water, for example, is that it is both powerful and soft at the same time. It takes life and it gives life. The sound of its trickle soothes us and its cool pure taste refreshes us on a hot day. Our bodies require water to survive. But over time the powerful force of water can cut through rock and carve miles of ravines like the Grand Canyon. The force of water can generate electricity and the force of its floods can destroy property and even life. Thus the yin and yang of water is that it is simultaneously life-sustaining and life-threatening. So even the opposites in life are one and the same.

The fact that both physicists and mystics endorse the concept of oneness lends support to the Principle of the Boomerang. Therefore if we're all one, every time we help someone else, we help to heal ourselves. By the same token, every time we hurt someone else, we simultaneously hurt ourselves.

When we send out destructive words and actions, our negative energy returns in some form to hurt us because of this oneness. Every time we send ourselves negative thoughts or put ourselves down in any way, we have injured others. We transfer self-injury into daily relationships by hurting others. When we love ourselves first and foremost, we transfer that self-love into caring and helping those around us. Expressions of love start now with loving ourselves.

Weapons Of The Tongue

Tongue-lashing, biting sarcasm, spiteful gossip, cutting cynicism. The tongue is a powerful and sharp sword that can cut, disfigure and cripple the human spirit. We can do more damage to others and ourselves with hateful comments than with a nuclear bomb. Ugly remarks can slice the human spirit into a million pieces in half the time it takes to put bullets into a gun.

The tongue is also a miracle healer, for it is through interactions with one another that we find answers in our healing quest. Kind words, gentle reminders, loving affirmations, soft reassurances and affectionate support can do as much to soothe and mend an injured spirit as human medicine.

How do *we* use our tongues? Do we denounce ourselves and others? Do we condemn, incapacitate, humiliate, embarrass and disgrace? Or do we uplift, heal, support, inspire and restore ourselves and others with healing words?

Using the 10 Principles of Healing for our own selfish gain or to hurt others will come back to us. Shakti Gawain explains, "Whatever you try to create for another will always boomerang back to you. That includes both loving, helpful or healing actions and negative destructive ones." So the more we use our thoughts, feelings and actions to love ourselves and others and do kind deeds, the more love, happiness and prosperity we will receive.

Step 12 of the 12 Steps says, *"Having had a spiritual awakening as the result of these steps, we tried to carry this message to others and to practice these principles in all our affairs."* In culmination of the other steps, we return what we have received back to the universe. We give freely of ourselves, not out of obligation but out of love. We may get involved with an employee assistance program at work, volunteer our help in a center for the homeless, lead a clean-up campaign in our neighborhood, take a new employee under our wing or we may live our lives by example.

Putting all the principles into practice helps us connect from the heart instead of just the head. Relationships become healthier, and positive people come into our lives. We radiate and attract people through our deeds and actions, and we become positive role models for others. We share (without preaching, lecturing or advising) our healing experiences with those who want to know.

As we share our message with others, we touch and help them transform their lives as we did ours. Hearing their message helps us on our own recovery path. The cycle perpetuates itself. As we share our conscious awakenings, we send out positive energy that helps others transform their lives. This, in turn, comes back to enrich our own lives a thousandfold.

Our Emotions As Boomerangs

All of our unhappiness and suffering come from our addictive way of thinking. No one else is to blame for our mental mindsets. When we are bothered by someone's way of making bread or of driving a car, *we* are the ones who need readjusting, not them. Negatively reacting to someone else, whose reality doesn't match our own, boomerangs back to us. Trying to make them do things our way violates the Principle of Harmony and creates frustration for ourselves. Our frustration can set up a chain reaction that causes others to respond to us in negative ways, bringing us additional hurt and upset.

On a physical level, body chemistry research of the 1990s shows that our own emotions act as boomerangs. Negative thoughts always create negative emotions, and negative emotions unleash biochemical enzymes in the body that create destructive physical side effects. Positive thoughts, on the other hand, always create positive emotions and positive emotions create body chemistry that has beneficial physical side effects.

Stress psychologist Hans Selye long ago told how the body manufactures its own poisons when under siege by negative emotions. It is possible for us to become recipients of the effects of our own frustration, anger or rage. Our anger can kill us and our laughter can heal and sustain us. Negative dark moods have harmful physical effects on our bodies, causing our body chemistry to secrete chemicals that do us danger. Happy joyful moods have positive effects on our bodies.

Norman Cousins, in his book *Headfirst*, declares, "Scarcely anything that enters the mind doesn't find its way into the workings of the body."

There is a whole world of body chemistry going on inside us. Our output, such as emotions, reactions and attitudes, creates accompanying inner physiological change. Positive output leads to positive input; our body chemistry responds in a positive way. So positive emotions provide an antidote to buffer disease. Negative output causes our inner workings to respond in a like manner, essentially doing harm to us and possibly even contributing to our ultimate demise. Changing old addictive thinking patterns to healing patterns sets up a chain reaction, and we receive a healthy dose of physical side effects.

Biochemical evidence from the laboratory shows that our negative emotions can ricochet on us to cause ourselves harm, and we may never realize it until it is too late. Anger and hostility cause the release of the hormone epinephrine which makes the heart beat fast and blood pressure rise. High blood pressure leads to damaged arteries and heart attack.

Long-standing research also links workaholism to the release of adrenalin in the body. Adrenalin is a hormone produced by the body in times of stress that has a similar effect as amphetamines or "speed." Psychologists believe that compulsive workers unconsciously put themselves under stressful situations to get the body to pump its fix. Workaholics often describe a surge of energy pumping through their veins and accompanying euphoria from the "adrenalin high." Addicted to adrenalin, workaholics require larger doses to maintain the high that they create by putting themselves and those around them under stress.

Adrenalin addiction, in effect, creates addictions to crises so that the body will produce the hormone and workaholics will get their drug. On the job, workaholics routinely create and douse crises, which require the body's adrenalin flow. While they get high, co-workers and subordinates experience many of the same emotions as children of alcoholics, notably unpredictability, confusion and frustration. These interpersonal difficulties, in turn, come back to the workaholic who must face them. The adrenalin flow also boomerangs in the form of physical problems. Too much adrenalin blocks the cell's ability to clear dangerous cholesterol from the bloodstream. Elevations of cholesterol clog arteries, damage their inner lining and can cause heart attacks.

We know too that high stress and negative feelings have been linked to other body chemistry changes that are believed to produce cancerous cells. Positive attitudes activate forces in the endocrine system and enhance the immune system. One study, for example, reveals that newly-separated and divorced men and women have a lower number of T-cells (the part of the immune system that fights off foreign invaders) due to accompanying stress than married couples of comparable age and background. Research also shows that reduction of stress and increase of positive emotions have the effect of boosting the immune system.

Norman Cousins reports research in the newly-developing field of psychoneuroimmunology — a branch of medicine at UCLA based on the interaction of the brain, the endocrine system and the immune system — which has revealed the beneficial effects of laughter on the immune system. Body chemistry research indicates that positive feelings, such as laughter and optimism, enhance the immune system by increasing the number of disease-fighting immune cells. Laughter also activates the secretion of endorphins, the body's own pain killer, that help reduce physical pain. Humor and mirth generally reduce stress, ease pain, foster recovery and generally brighten one's outlook on life, regardless of how grim the reality. When we send out positive feelings, we get back actual physical benefits that can prolong and improve the quality of our lives.

Those of us who persist in angry outbursts and hostility against others, says the Principle of the Boomerang, are ultimately hurting ourselves. Holding on to anger and resentment has a boomerang effect and hurts us a lot more than the ones toward whom we direct our wrath. When we harbor negative feelings, we literally turn them inward upon ourselves where they do us emotional and physical harm. They ravage the nervous, digestive, cardiac and respiratory systems. Worst of all, they stand in the way of our spiritual healing and keep us stuck in misery and defeat.

Many times our depressed emotional states boomerang on us in the form of poor health because of weakened immune systems. During the course of my own breakup of the relationship I had before the prophetic experience on the Jamaican beach, I became very sick with the first case of flu in ten years. I slept for a solid week. I am convinced that my depression and negativism lowered my immune system and contributed to my susceptibility to the virus. My negative emotional state, in effect, created my negative circumstances in the form of poor health. Addictive thinking, feeling and behaving over prolonged periods of time ricochet and become hazardous to our health.

In the words of Catherine Ponder, author of *The Dynamic Laws of Prosperity:*

"It is up to you to dare to choose and radiate outward through your thinking what you really wish to experience in life, rather than to get bogged down in unpleasant or failure experiences of the moment. These conditions can change as quickly as you can change your thinking about them."

Turning anger into love unblocks the spiritual path and heads us back in the right direction.

The Boomerang Activity

We do not send out positive energy for the sole purpose of getting something in return. We follow the Principle of the Boomerang because of a genuine self-love and love for others. We send out positive vibrations without regard for personal gain. What good would you like to put forth without regard for material gain? Below you can set some personal goals in each of the designated areas.

1. I will send positive thoughts to someone today. State the person and the thought. _____

_____

_____

_____

2. I will say something constructive to someone today. State the person and the words. _____

_____

_____

_____

3. I will feel something good toward someone today. State the person and the feelings. _____

_____

_____

_____

4. I will do a kind deed for someone today. State the person and the actions. _____

_____

_____

_____

Once you have actually achieved the four goals, identify your feelings. Chances are that your boomerang has already come back to you through the realization that "giving is as fulfilling as receiving." You can build giving and helping into your life on a regular basis by acting as a volunteer worker for a favorite organization, sponsoring a needy child from a developing country, donating to charities or lending a helping hand to someone in need. Sharing your thoughts and feelings with those who are downtrodden helps them and you grow by leaps and bounds. As you give, you receive. As you bestow, you acquire. As you share, you prosper. All the spiritual riches of the universe will come to you as you practice these principles in your daily affairs.

Use the space below to record your thoughts and feelings.

CHAPTER 11

Birds of a feather flock together.

Miguel de Cervantes

The Principle
Of Magnetism

We attract people into our lives who think, feel and behave like us and thus people closest to us are mirrors of ourselves.

"Tell me why I keep getting involved in relationships with men who use me and then reject me," Sharon demanded.

When Sharon did something wrong as a child, she had to win back her mother's approval. Her mother gave her the cold shoulder until she proved she could be the perfect little girl. Today that perfect little girl is attracted to co-dependent relationships and men who psychologically reject her. Sharon relives the relationship with her mother many times over by making herself a doormat for the men she dates so they will love and approve of her. She attends Co-dependents Anonymous to help her understand that there is nothing wrong with her and that she doesn't need another person to make her complete.

At age 44 Phyllis couldn't understand why her life was not working. She was miserable and everyone in her life seemed to contribute to her misery. She was a severe workaholic with three Ph.Ds. She was compulsively in control of herself and everyone around her. Her husband was also a workaholic who barely spoke to her. They had not had an intimate relationship for 12 years. Phyllis's father died an alcoholic. Her sister and brother were both active alcoholics. "I continue to attract and am attracted to losers," she mourned. "Why isn't my life working?"

Another woman said, "Every man I have fallen in love with has abused me."

Kyle, who is the son of an alcoholic, declared half seriously and half jokingly, "I can be the only man in a room with 100 women, only one of whom is an adult child from a dysfunctional family, and we gravitate straight toward each other in five minutes flat!"

Like Attracts Like

These scenarios are told again and again all over the United States. We can explain this phenomenon by the Principle of Magnetism or mutual attraction: Like attracts like.

On a metaphysical level, this law of mutual attraction is explained through the interaction of subatomic particles that are all around us. Each of us has an energy field. We are walking, talking, electrical fields of energy that seek harmony. The frequencies of our magnetic fields are pulled in various directions toward other compatible fields of energy. We are drawn toward people who have compatible energy fields. Thoughts and feelings have their own magnetic energy that attract energy of a similar nature. So when we put one adult child in a room with 100 people, only one of whom is an adult child, the two will gravitate toward one another.

Addictive thinkers give off energy of a particular quality and frequency that attracts the one other adult child in a crowd because that other adult is also radiating energy of a similar frequency and vibration. As we learn to change old distorted thoughts and feelings, we literally change the frequency and vibration of our energy fields, so that we no longer attract and are no longer attracted to dysfunctional relationships.

A wealth of psychological research also exists that shows conclusively how like attracts like. Children of alcoholics, for example, are four times more likely to become alcoholics themselves than children from nonalcoholic homes. Of course, genetic factors are in play here to some extent. But the dynamic family relationships contribute a large role to this intergenerational trend.

The magnetic pattern clearly is seen in the types of relationships children from dysfunctional homes form in adulthood. Statistics indicate that adults from alcoholic homes tend to marry and become friends with other adult children from dysfunctional homes. Or they are attracted to and marry spouses who are co-dependent or alcoholic, thereby replicating the dysfunction from their families of origin. Adult children may become alcoholic, marry alcoholics and often surround themselves with friends and co-workers who also came from dysfunctional families and who have some type of addiction to drugs, food, work, sex, relationships and so forth.

Fatal Attraction

This is the Principle of Magnetism. We are attracted to friends, loved ones and family members who are like us. Our thoughts mold the character of our lives, and we create our life conditions by what we think. What we believe comes true for us. Addictive thinkers are attracted to other addictive thinkers because they perceive life in similar ways. As a result, their emotions and behaviors are compatible. Their addictive thinking patterns fit together like a hand and glove. As we surround ourselves with people like us, we replay over and over again the addictive thinking from our past. It feels familiar. It's all we know. And we are not even conscious that we have surrounded ourselves with other people who think in addictive ways.

If we dislike ourselves, we tend to be attracted to others who dislike themselves and express it through unkind deeds. When we are troubled and confused, we are attracted to troubled and disturbed personalities. If we are not kind to ourselves, chances are that our friends and loved ones are not kind to us either.

We unconsciously surround ourselves with people with whom we feel comfortable and familiar. Perhaps we are attracted to friends and lovers, even business associates, for whom we feel sorry or who need us to help them live their lives. We may come to realize that we are surrounded by co-dependent refugees who we have rescued in our personal and professional lives.

There is an old saying, "When you lie down with dogs, you get up with fleas." The company we keep rubs off on us, and we on them. We influence each other's thoughts and behaviors through a reciprocal cycle of interaction. Some of us even become addicted to chronic caretaking which keeps the focus off ourselves and on someone else. We may hear a lecture or read something and think, "Now this is what my wife or husband or friend needs to hear." Getting sidetracked on others causes us to miss an opportunity to learn from what we experience. We have a natural high when watching a breathtaking sunset and think, "If only I had someone with whom to enjoy this." We spend so much time saving others that we neglect ourselves and miss important opportunities for our own personal growth. The person needing rescuing is us. The 10 Principles of Healing teach us to rescue ourselves from our own co-dependency and careaholism. We can do this by evaluating the company we keep. Do we seek relationships with people who devalue our worth or ones who mirror and affirm our true value?

Your Magnetogram

You can trace the types of people that are drawn into your life. A *magnetogram* is a map of your magnetic tree . . . the close relationships that you form through mutual attraction with the important people in your life.

STEP ONE:

Begin by filling in the blanks below.
1. Put your name here: _____

2. Put your parents' names here:
   (Mother) _____
   (Father) _____

3. Name up to two current or former spouses or major love interests:

   _____
   _____

4. List two family members with whom you are closest. These can be your brothers, sisters, relatives or your children:

   _____
   _____

5. List your two closest friends whom you see regularly:

   _____
   _____

6. Identify up to two co-workers with whom you *choose* to spend the most time on the job:

   _____
   _____

STEP TWO:
Once you have filled in all the blanks, put beside each name the symbol from below that stands for any addictive experience that person (including yourself) has had. Each name can have more than one symbol beside it.

Addictive Symbols
   A = alcohol or other drug problems
   E = eating disorders
   W = work addiction
   R = co-dependent or addictive relationships
   P = physical abusers or physically abused
   I = incest abusers or incest survivors
   O = any other identifiable addictive habit, behavior or experience

STEP THREE:
Plot the results of your magnetogram by putting the addictive symbols from above inside the appropriate geo-

metric shapes below. The center circle represents you.
Begin by putting any addictive symbols for yourself inside
the circle. Then continue putting the addictive symbols in
the geometric shapes that surround you. The following
geometric shapes represent the people closest to you:

Relationship Symbols

☐ = parents

⬡ = spouse/love interest

○ = family members

△ = friends

⬡ = co-workers

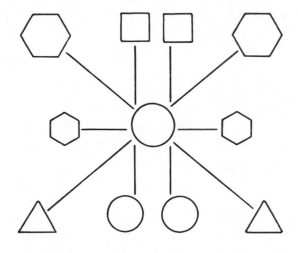

The point of this exercise is not to get you to feel
guilty or bad about yourself but to help you get an objective view of your life. The magnetogram helps you take
an honest look at the context of your life but asks that
you not blame or condemn yourself or anyone else for
what you see. You may feel you have created an addictive life by surrounding yourself with addictive-thinking

people. In many instances we continue surrounding ourselves with people who mirror our own unworthiness, a
picture consistent with our childhood image of ourselves.

Think about the following questions that relate to your
magnetogram: What kinds of people surround you in
your life? Do they replay old unhealthy voices reminding
you of how unworthy you are? Do they humiliate and
condemn you? Or do they support and affirm you? What
does this tell you about yourself and your relationships?
Are there relationship patterns you'd like to change? If
so, which ones and how can you accomplish this change
in a positive and healthy way?

Setting Boundaries

The Principle of Magnetism is working against us
when we are so strongly drawn to other persons that we
cling and lose our identity in them. These unhealthy at-
tachments are called *co-dependent relationships*. Co-dependents are like vacuum cleaners because they draw to
themselves other people, substances or processes to fill
the great emptiness they feel within themselves. Those
of us with unmet emotional needs attract others like
ourselves to fill up that inner gap. Often we are unconsciously attracted to the types of people who have the
same addictive traits that we are trying to shed. We enter
relationships to rescue each other, to feel more complete
in each other's embrace, to take refuge from the world.
We merge our needy lives so tightly that we relinquish all
sense of independence and individuality. We become so
intertwined that we become addicted to each other. We
become dependent upon each other for self-esteem and
all our emotional needs.

Mutual Attraction With Separate Boundaries

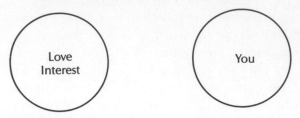

Drawn Together In The Beginning Of The Relationship

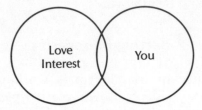

Loss of Personal Boundaries In Co-dependent Relationship

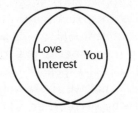

Re-establishment Of Healthy Boundaries

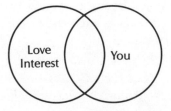

Figure 11.1. Relationship Boundaries

How many times have we heard the phrases, "Don't rock the boat," "Don't change," or "Don't make trouble." Leave things as they are. Don't interfere with things the way others want them. Sacrifice. The messages have been branded into our brains to keep peace at all costs, even at the expense of our own happiness and sanity.

Such was the case of Ralph, who left a 16-year marriage with three kids. Ralph was a people-pleaser who couldn't make even the simplest decisions on his own. He had no opinions, attitudes or preferences and depended on his wife, Marcy, to decide when and what to eat, who their friends were and when and where to go on vacation. Ralph had no sense of self because he lived his life for everyone else. The family was inseparable. When one member went to K-Mart, the whole family had to go.

Unexpectedly one day Ralph announced his deep unhappiness to Marcy, who was shocked beyond belief. She thought they had the "perfect" relationship. She ran the show and Ralph did what he was told. Now Ralph told her, "I don't know who I am anymore. I feel dead inside. I want out of this marriage." Marcy tried to convince him otherwise. But Ralph, in his attempts to take his first stand and not lose the upper hand declared, "My mind is made up. Don't try to change it. There's no hope for this marriage. I want to divorce and sell the house."

Marcy, who felt victimized, presented her problem to me as, "Ralph walked out on us." Marcy wanted to know what she could do to help Ralph with his co-dependency and help him see the light. I suggested that she let Ralph work on Ralph and that she work on *her* issues. Stunned, she asked, "What do you mean? I don't have a problem." To which I responded, "What did it feel like having to make all the decisions for three kids and an adult for 16 years every day of your life?" She acknowledged that it was draining and tiresome and that for the first time in her life she felt a weight had been lifted from her shoulders.

After additional probing, Marcy admitted anger over always having to be emotionally responsible for a husband who couldn't accept responsibility. The more we talked, the clearer it became that Marcy had many issues of her own that she needed to work through. Both parties in this relationship were bound together by their addictive thinking which manifested itself through co-dependency.

As we start to heal from co-dependency, sometimes we rock the boat a little, as Ralph did. But we do not deliberately cause confusion just to be hostile. As we get healthier, we begin to assert ourselves and to set boundaries. Speaking up for ourselves breaks established addictive patterns. Co-workers, loved ones and friends who are not used to our standing up for what we need may be somewhat surprised, even shaken by our change. The boat sways, rocks and a few might even sink. Those around us may reel from the change.

But as we begin speaking up, standing firm and taking care of ourselves, we don't have to let another's discomfort cause us to back down. We are deserving and worthy too. When the boat rocks, that's not our fault. We can rely on our healing process. The rocking boat will stabilize on its own as will everyone affected by it.

Everybody needs boundaries to grow. Boundaries tell us how far we can go. They keep us from overstepping. Small children have the best learning opportunities when they have limits within which to learn and explore. A backyard fence is the best thing for toddlers because it keeps them safe and healthy. Like the backyard fence, boundaries keep us mentally safe and healthy in our personal relationships.

Boundaries are essential if we are to remain separate human beings. They allow us to keep our individuality and uniqueness. Our likes and dislikes do not get confused and ensnared with those of someone close to us. We don't have to give up chocolate just because someone else likes vanilla. We don't have to move from the shade just because they like the sun. Boundaries help us to own our feelings and thoughts and accept responsibility for our mistakes and growth. Boundaries don't keep people out; they let them know how far in they can come.

Those of us who are chronic caretakers, like Marcy, begin to draw boundaries and stop feeling responsible for whatever happens around us. We stop blaming ourselves when situations go haywire and we have no control over them. We stop apologizing for things that are not our fault. We don't feel we have failed when we haven't saved the world. We don't feel the emotions that someone else needs to feel. And our self-contempt and guilt over not being superhuman evaporate. As we allow ourselves to be human with all its fallibilities and strengths, we practice the art of self-care.

Barricades Versus Boundaries

Sharing ourselves in relationships is not as easy as it sounds. We've had to protect and pretend for so long in our relationships that being intimate is a problem for many of us from dysfunctional homes. We often get confused between setting boundaries in relationships and shutting others out.

Expressing intimacy teaches us the difference between establishing boundaries and erecting barricades. Boundaries define how far we go; barricades prevent us from going anywhere. Sometimes as we drop our barricades, we drop our boundaries, too, and get involved in co-dependent relationships. We lose our identity in someone else's life and let them manipulate and control us. We replace alienation with co-dependent relationships, both of which isolate us from ourselves. Without our boundaries, we are just as isolated as we were with our barricades.

Personal healing teaches us to gradually remove the barricades while simultaneously keeping boundaries. We open our minds and hearts and share ourselves with other people. But we keep self-respect and individuality because intimacy always requires that we draw a fine line.

How tragic it would be if our personalities melted together with each person we met. We would become one great glob. But how tragic, too, if we never revealed and shared ourselves with another human being. As we heal, we are able to share ourselves as we genuinely are — both the good and the bad, the strengths and faults, successes and mistakes. One of the miracles of healing is to trust enough to remove barricades. How wondrous to stand together, to love and support one another with clear boundaries.

Detachment

One way to accomplish clear boundaries is through detachment. Sometimes the negativity of co-workers, family members or friends pulls us down. Perhaps we feel uncomfortable with a colleague's jeers at a co-worker. A neighbor engages in vindictive gossip about the people next door. A spouse, lover or roommate comes home ranting and raving about a bad day at work. We care about the colleague, neighbor and loved one but feel that our mental health is being affected by their insults, sarcasm or gossip. We can have love and compassion for those closest to us without loving what they do.

When people or situations become too much for us, we can detach ourselves while maintaining our love for them. Detachment might mean physically removing ourselves temporarily from a situation or just holding our tongues and remaining silent. In either case we detach with love, not with anger. Through the power of detachment, we are able to perceive situations more clearly, maintain our serenity, love unconditionally and continue to radiate joy and peace to everyone. We do not have to take on the problems and negativity of those around us. But our compassion and love for their welfare is unyielding. We can always detach ourselves from destructive feelings that hinder our own growth.

We sometimes need to detach ourselves from loved ones and colleagues so that their negativity or problems do not divert us from our own healing journey. Many of us unwittingly become obsessed and consumed in other people's problems at the expense of neglecting our own. We are so accustomed to being the controller or the mediator that it is hard to resist the urge to fix other people's problems, even while our own lives are in complete shambles.

Detachment is neither kind nor unkind. It allows us to put our own house in order first. It does not mean that we are insensitive or emotionless or that we do not have compassion. But it enables us to work on ourselves without distraction. Detachment without amputation allows us to be objective and to keep from getting enmeshed in problems over which we have no control.

When situations interfere with our own personal healing, detachment without amputation allows us to remove ourselves, either physically or emotionally, from unhealthy situations out of love — not out of anger or resentment. We can love and help those we are attracted to only as much as we love and help ourselves. It is important to address our needs first and get our own lives in order before offering a helping hand to others.

Circle Of Healing

Ralph and Marcy's old relationship was dead. Ralph pursued a course of change that Marcy's old role no longer fit. According to the Principle of Magnetism, the only way for relationships to survive is for both parties to be headed in the same direction of change: like attracts like. Odds are that if Ralph remained co-dependent and Marcy stayed in the old addictive patterns, the marriage would plod along. But as Ralph began to assert himself and work on his co-dependent issues, the survival of the marriage required that Marcy change too. As Ralph changes his addictive thinking about himself and his relationships, Marcy's attempts to control and manipulate his behaviors only push him farther away. Hope for Ralph and Marcy comes as they both embark on their separate healing journeys. Changing their addictive thinking helps them recognize the death of their addictive relationship and the rebirth of a healthier one.

As we start to get healthier, our relationships automatically undergo change. We find it almost impossible to remain in relationships with others who continue their addictive thinking and behaving. Addictive thinkers have attitudes, feelings and actions that rub us the wrong way and negate newly-found healthy thinking. The patterns become clear, and we are repelled rather than attracted to their addictive energy because we have changed.

The old ways no longer feel comfortable or healthy. It's like trying to wear old clothes that don't fit. Friends and co-workers often think someone who is healing themselves is a "weirdo" or is going through a midlife crisis. They may start to distance themselves because they feel threatened. Remember, we live in a society where it is still considered strange to sit cross-legged, close your eyes and meditate. But it is considered normal to party, get rip-roaring drunk, whoop and holler, and crawl around on all fours.

The Principle of Magnetism holds that like attracts like. When two people in a relationship both abide by core beliefs of addictive thinking, the relationship can survive. When two people in a relationship are both following the 10 Principles of Healing, the relationship can survive. But when one person in a relationship continues addictive living and the other person is healing his or her addictive thoughts, there is no hope for the relationship to survive. It's like water and oil. The magnetic chemistry doesn't mix.

As we obey the 10 Principles of Healing, we may find ourselves giving up old relationships and drawn to new and healthier ones. We have simply begun to attract and become attracted to healthier people in our lives.

In my own personal growth I found myself repelled by relationships based on addictive thinking. I started to attract and become attracted to healthier relationships. It was difficult for me to tolerate the addictive thinking and actions of close friends who seemed content to stay in that spot. By the same token, some friends who didn't understand the change in me, who were threatened by it, began to distance themselves. In their place, I connected with old friends who continued a healing journey similar to mine and I established new and meaningful relationships with others whom I met in recovery.

When we look beneath the reason for our clinging to others who are unhealthy for us, we discover that we're often reliving childhood relationships many times over. Perhaps we continue to get involved in relationships with those who emotionally reject us. Or we make ourselves a doormat for others so that they will love and approve of us.

Once we resolve the old feelings we're trying to work out with new people today, we heal our compulsive need for love and approval. The solution is self-love. We stop beating ourselves up. We stop bringing people into our lives who wipe their feet on us. We get to know ourselves. We practice self acceptance and self-approval. We affirm and pamper ourselves. We concentrate on ourselves with attention and nurturance of which we have deprived ourselves for so long. We support, forgive and care for ourselves to the hilt. We enjoy our own company and become our own best friend.

The Magnetic Exercise

Think of yourself as an irresistible magnet, capable of attracting all the good that surrounds you: healthy positive relationships, joy, happiness and serenity. Radiate positive thoughts and feelings. Think only good things happening for everyone you know — those closest to you and even those you feel at odds with. Fill your mind with healthy thoughts and image good things for yourself. As you radiate positive thoughts, visualize positive things drawn toward you. See yourself attracting whatever you radiate.

As you practice self-love, co-dependent relationships melt away. Breaking your attraction to unhealthy relationships begins with your own self-acceptance and self-love. Then it spreads, like concentric circles on a rippling pond, to your immediate circle of relationships. The outer ripples continue to touch those at work and in your circle of business associates and acquaintances. You radiate care, love and healing wherever you go and attract (and are attracted to) people who are spreading the same positive energy to you. You avoid others who minimize your value and detract from your personal healing and keep the company of affirming people. You find yourself surrounded with other people who love and care for themselves and who mirror your own inner beauty and self-worth. Say the following affirmation to yourself: *"I am a healthy, loving, happy person and I attract healthy, loving and happy people."*

CHAPTER 12

*We believe that everything there is to find is out there in the light where it's easy to find, when the only answers for **you** are in **you!***

Leo Buscaglia

The Principle Of The Inner Guru

Healing addictive thoughts and lifestyles comes from the inside out, not the outside in.

Twenty-two-year-old Sheila worked for a computer company in New York City. She was bored and weary of the grind of morning rush hours, daily routines and afternoon traffic jams. She had few friends and was generally unhappy with her life. Finally, with her mother's encouragement, Sheila decided to go to California to "find herself." After a few months, she decided that Los Angeles "was not what it is cracked up to be" so she moved to Seattle.

The Outer Journey

Unfortunately geographic escape doesn't help us find ourselves. Our inner selves are not waiting on some faraway street corner for our bodies to catch up with them. We simply pack up our old habits and carry them like luggage wherever we go. The surroundings are different but our responses are the same. If we wake up feeling positive and optimistic in Detroit, we wake up feeling positive and optimistic in the Mediterranean. If we awaken to anxiety and pessimism in Buffalo, we wake up to anxiety and pessimism in the South Pacific. The grass is not greener in another spot. Those of us who feel incomplete and unfinished often look outside ourselves to fill the void. We stuff it with projects, computer printouts, deadlines, unhealthy relationships and material possessions. We become addicted to acquiring power and get consumed with making it to the top. We aim for worldly achievements, approval and financial rewards. We become enslaved by greed, competition and material gain as we try to heal our past insecurities and addictive thinking.

We search frantically for purpose in our daily lives through our jobs, our relationships, our drugs, our cars or our homes. We expect our careers, our kids, our love interests or the expert books and gurus to heal us. We become co-dependent with some outside person, some thing or some growth movement that we expect will bring self-fulfillment. We look in the wrong place when we search outside ourselves for purpose in life. We discover it when we look within and connect with our own inner guru.

Joseph Campbell said,

> "We're so engaged in doing things to achieve purposes of outer value but the inner value, the rapture that is associated with being alive, is what it's all about."

We are often so busy "getting there," we forget we are already "there" and that there is nowhere else to go. Ourselves is all we really have, and discovering the treasure of self is the key to the Principle of the Inner Guru. All we need do is look within. We don't have to rush to get ahead because we already are ahead when we connect with our innermost self. Only by inner transformation do we make a significant change that can improve the quality of our lives.

The Inner Journey

As we connect with our inner selves we have a conscious awakening that makes us complete and nurtures us with purpose and meaning. The inner connection is a perpetual journey that we never finish. The only way to finish a spiritual life is to be ever beginning it each day. We never stop healing ourselves, and we never arrive anywhere on our spiritual path. We progress as we grow more and more with each new day.

We find a piece of gold at the end of each day's rainbow on this perpetual treasure hunt. We discover new and exciting things about ourselves as each day unfolds. We unravel the mystery that surrounds our lives, and we find beauty in the ordinary, elegance in the simple, wisdom in the shallow and excitement in the commonplace. We exchange material possessions for spiritual ways and learn to diminish our wants rather than increase our needs.

This process hinges on the Principle of the Inner Guru because all the change takes place inside you, not in the outside world. This means that much of your practice and work must occur in your mind and heart.

The only way to change someone else is to change yourself.

Recovery comes from realizing that we cannot control anyone or anything but ourselves and that we can be responsible only for ourselves.

You can rearrange your furniture, change jobs, divorce and remarry, establish new friendships, buy a new wardrobe, move to another state, color your hair, buy a new car, build a new house, have a child, get high from your favorite addiction and on and on. But these are all futile efforts at changing your co-dependent thoughts and feelings so that you can be happy. These changes are exterior changes and have no lasting effect. The source of healing lies within the self, not outside the self.

As you persist looking outside yourself for happiness, you are, as the Buddhist example suggests, like the man searching for his lost ox who doesn't realize he is already mounted on its back.

Josh Billings gives us a more westernized version: "If you ever find happiness by hunting for it, you will find it, as the old woman did her lost spectacles, safe on her own nose all the time!"

Only through interior change will you find the answers you have been looking for. The answers are not out there; they are inside of you. Everything comes from the way you think about yourself. If you want to change your life, you must change the way you think about yourself first. Everything else follows.

Addictive thinking makes it easier to accept the bad than the good because that fits more with how you think of yourself. Most people feel more comfort with criticism and put-downs than praise. The Principle of the Inner Guru says that you must begin to accept your own good. Accepting your own good is a way of accepting the truth about yourself. Seeing yourself honestly includes acknowledging and affirming all the good things about yourself. You love yourself with no strings attached. You learn to allow yourself to make mistakes, to forgive yourself for those mistakes, and to go on with your life. You let those perfectionistic standards drop a little. When you put conditions on loving yourself and others, you keep yourself stuck in addictive thinking.

Inner healing occurs only through unconditional love. When you see yourself as a worthy, loving and competent human being, others begin to treat you that way and the world operates that way for you. Harmony in the world begins with harmonizing yourself from within. You allow yourself to be led from within once you realize that you are your own best guru. That's why "guru" is spelled "Gee-You-Are-You."

Healograms

Healograms are visual roadmaps that give us direction on our healing journey. I created them to help us see those areas of our lives in which we are putting our healing energies. They tell us whether we seek healing in the *outer* world of career, recreation and relationships or in the *inner* world of self and spiritual needs. Healograms give us a graphic picture of the life areas in which we focus our energies, those that we have overlooked and those in which we can put more time and energy for a more fulfilling life.

Figure 12.1 shows samples of the "Healogram As I Am Now" and "Healogram As I Would Like To Be." Notice that the man who filled out this healogram would like to spend less time working and more time on spiritual, self and relationship pursuits. Figure 12.2 contains the Healograms that are to be completed by you. Begin with "My Healogram As I Am Now." Choose one of the five areas listed on the healogram in which you spend *most* of your time and energy. Above that area draw a verticle line which will be the highest line in the graph. Next consider the area in which you spend the *least* amount of time and energy. Above that area, draw a vertical line that will be the shortest line in the graph to represent this area. Then fill in the other lines that correspond to the proportionate amount of time that you spend in each of the remaining three areas of life. Follow the same directions using vertical lines for "My Healogram As I Would Like To Be." The differences between the "My Healogram As I Am Now" and "My Healogram As I Would Like To Be" are your goals for healing. This identifies the areas in which you can focus on your healing work. There are no right or wrong answers. The usefulness of the Healograms is all in how *you* see it.

Sample Healogram As I Am Now

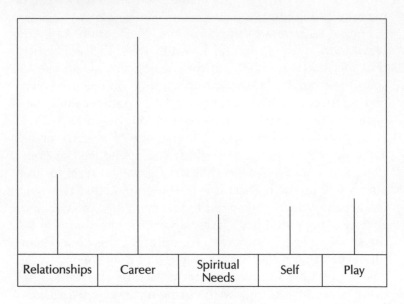

Sample Healogram As I Would Like To Be

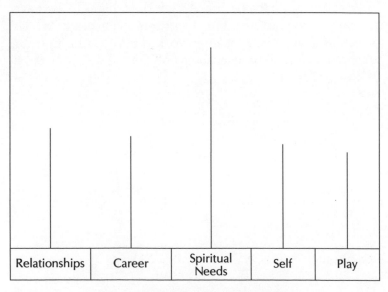

Figure 12.1. Sample Healograms

My Healogram As I Am Now

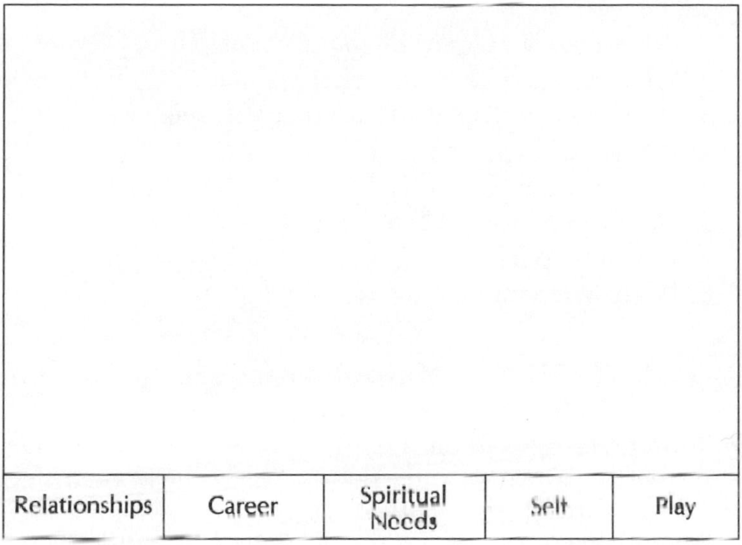

Relationships	Career	Spiritual Needs	Self	Play

My Healogram As I Would Like To Be

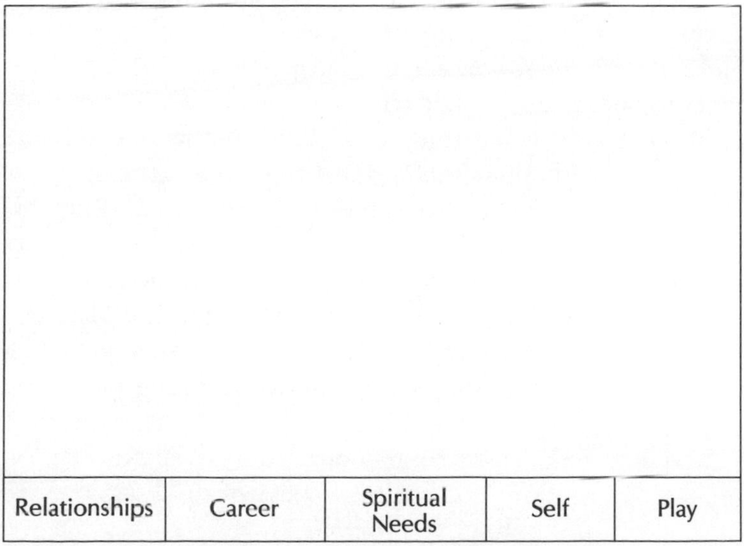

Relationships	Career	Spiritual Needs	Self	Play

Figure 12.2. My Healograms

After completing the Healograms, respond to the following questions:

1. What have you learned about yourself?
2. What do you like about what you see?
3. What do you dislike about what you see?
4. What could you change?
5. Do you want to change?
6. How would you do that?
7. Will you do it?
8. When will you begin?

Formula For Healing Yourself From The Inside Out

If misery is created on the inside, doesn't it make sense that the first step is to start there? The focus of recovery is on *inner* life, not *outer* life. Change your thinking and you change your life. Abandon the addictive thinking and replace it with healing eyes, and unhappiness disappears and eternal happiness is yours.

When you are unhappy or things are not going right, ask yourself which of the 10 Principles of Healing you are violating. You can correct the old patterns with the formula for healing yourself from the inside out.

Stage 1: You learn that addictive thinking comes from addictive perceptions that you developed in childhood through the eyes of your caregivers. *(Principle 1)*

Stage 2: You recognize that your life is in the condition that it is now because of your continued addictive thinking and that you can change your life by changing your addictive thinking patterns. *(Principle 2)*

Stage 3: You decide to abandon your addictive way of thinking for healthier ways of thinking, feeling and behaving. *(Principle 3)*

Stage 4: You practice the Principle of Healing through optimism, positive expectations, harmony, empowerment, radiation and attraction. *(Principles 4, 5, 6, 7, 8 and 9)*

Stage 5: You replace addictive thinking and living with a healing approach to life based on unconditional love and forgiveness and commit yourself to an ongoing journey of personal growth by following these principles. *(Principle 10)*

A personal story of my own is one example of how you can apply this formula to your life. Before beginning my recovery from addictive thinking, I often had difficulty speaking before groups. Sometimes before I made a speech to hundreds of people, my inner addictive voice would speak to me. It told me how incompetent I was: "You don't know what you're talking about. You're going to mess up. People will go away disgruntled and disappointed." Hearing these inner messages made my stomach flip flop, and I would become anxious. I gave the addictive thinking my power and became victimized by it.

I became pessimistic and engaged in catastrophic thinking. I worried about "what if" I'm late or no one shows up or I forget what I am supposed to say. I unconsciously worked myself into a helpless state by believing the addictive thoughts. I disempowered myself with negative thinking that could sabotage the speech through negative expectations. I became so focused on externalized thinking and pleasing others that I abused myself with self-destructive thoughts. The night before a speech I couldn't eat, had difficulty sleeping and became short-tempered and withdrawn.

After a while I started to refuse public speaking engagements and did so for years. Being in recovery helped me to realize that my addictive thinking was controlling my life. That thinking caused negative emotions, such as frustration, worry and anxiety, which, in turn, caused addictive behaviors, such as withdrawal and irritability, and then I would seek refuge in overworking, chain-smoking and alcohol. Addictions begin with how we think, are transformed into feelings and manifested into behaviors.

We can even take this cycle a step further with the Principle of Expectation, which says that our addictive thoughts, feelings and behaviors (in this instance withdrawal and irritability) have a negative impact on those closest to us. Friends and loved ones may become annoyed with our sulking. We, in turn, perceive their annoyance as "insensitivity to our problems" and we react with hostility. So what begins as addictive thinking manifests itself through our negative actions and our interpersonal relationships.

Even in recovery the addictive voice still tries to hold conversations with me, especially before an event that might produce the slightest anxiety. That's when I apply the 10 Principle of Healing formula. I remind myself that my perception of this situation is addictive and that the voice is the addictive voice of my past. I remember that I do not have to listen to this voice anymore, because it *never* tells the truth. I remember that I have the power to change my apprehension simply by altering my perception of this situation. So I abandon the addictive voice and refuse to listen to it.

I go within and call forth my healing voice. The healing voice empowers me through optimism and gives me pep talks. It tells me, "You have never had a bad experience before. Why would you have one now? People continue to ask you back, and they are always complimentary. You get phone calls and letters from all over the nation from people who want to thank you for helping them."

The healing voice helps me rearrange my thinking. I remind myself that I am not doing this for reasons of self-aggrandizement but to help other people. I release the negative thoughts and let go of the negative feelings and think of my mind and heart as a vessel opened to the positive flow of the universe. I imagine my body being filled with this positive energy and visualize myself in harmony with it. My thoughts begin to take new form: "This will be an adventure. People are coming from all over to hear what I have to say. They will be able to take back valuable information that will help them change their own lives and the lives of others. I will gain something from them, too, that will teach me new lessons. This will be rewarding as well as fun. How exciting!"

I have come to realize through this process that addictive thinking is self-abusive. I was putting myself through mental torture. The 10 Principles of Healing help me intercept the self-abuse and love myself unconditionally. I treat myself with kindness and caring as I would anyone I care about. My self-love no longer allows the addictive thinking to bombard my emotional and immune system. I care too much for myself to allow myself to be abused as I was for so many years in my addictive family. Going through this process heals me of the addictive thoughts and feelings and I approach life with hope, optimism and happiness.

The Value Of Meditation

The purpose of meditation is to quiet the mind so that we can hear what is already there. It helps us look within, understand ourselves and establish inner harmony and balance so that we are more harmonious with the world and the people in it. Scientific research has shown that when we engage in visualizations and meditations, our whole body functions more slowly. Heart rate and brain wave patterns slow down when we are in meditative states. Going within through meditation has a positive effect on the immune system and body chemistry so that certain hormones are secreted that have life-sustaining qualities. Scientists have discovered that adults who meditate for a period of time each day actually live longer than adults who do not. In other words, the scientific world now appreciates the value of going within and connecting with the energy inside of ourselves.

The use of meditations and visualizations is a far more constructive and productive way of achieving our goals than worrying about "what if," trying to control situations that are beyond our control or getting upset and angry when things don't work out to suit us.

Guided visualizations give us a beginning structure for meditation. We receive guided instruction on what to visualize in step-by-step fashion. Guided visualizations are especially good for novices who are still developing their imagery capabilities. Practice is the key to successful visualization. The more you practice using your mental imagery, the sharper and more powerful your visualization will become.

Some beginners are afraid of going within. They are afraid of their feelings and facing emotions that are stored there. They are afraid that if they dredge up old feelings, they will open a floodgate and will never be able to stop crying once they start.

A woman in one of my seminars in Texas sat in the front row during a guided visualization that I conducted. She wrote frantically filling each page with words the entire time that the other participants experienced an inner journey. Later she apologized and said that she was afraid of what would happen if she took part. Her note-taking was simply a way of blocking any emotions from surfacing.

Going within and facing our hurt and pain is the only way we will ever heal. As long as we flee from our inner feelings, we can never resolve them. There is nothing within us that can harm us. We can only heal. Once we confront our deepest fears and experience them fully, they lose their power to dominate our thoughts.

Inner Guru Meditation

The following meditation can help you connect with your inner guru, the seat of all the answers to your problems. Get comfortable in a relaxed position and in a quiet place where you can put yourself fully into this journey. You may want to put this meditation on tape with soft music and play it back or have a friend guide you through.

Focus on your breathing. Take a few deep breaths. Let it all go. Get connected with your breathing.

Breathe in through the nose and out through the mouth, in through the nose and out through the mouth.

Feel the seat underneath you, feel the clothes on your body. Hear sounds around you. Let go of thoughts about what happened at work or at home today. Forget about what you have to do later today or tomorrow. This is a time for you.

As the thoughts race through your brain, don't resist them. Don't try to stop them. Just let them go. Let the thoughts pass through your mind. Acknowledge them and let them go. Don't hold on to any of them. Just let them pass on by. Continue your breathing. Relax.

Now go deep within yourself. Imagine yourself floating through the air. You're going on an inner journey and you can take someone with you on this journey, someone you are very close to: a child, a parent, a spouse, lover, friend or co-worker. It can be someone you see everyday. Or it can be someone you haven't seen in a long, long time, perhaps someone you thought you'd never see again. You can take anyone you wish, but only one.

Now, imagine that you're floating with your loved one through the air. You're floating in the clouds. You're as light as the clouds. Look around you. What do you see? Look below. What's there? Look beside you. Who's floating with you? Look at your companion. How does it feel to have this person with you? Now look above you. What do you see? What's in front of you? Imagine the wonder of it all in your mind's eye.

Pause for a while on a nearby cloud. Standing there look in the eyes of the person with you. This person cannot go with you any further. Say goodbye to your loved one. Say goodbye in any way you choose. You will make the rest of the journey on your own. Now say goodbye and let that person go.

Turn away and continue floating. Look back and see your loved one waving in the distance as you float away. Your loved one is getting smaller and smaller. How does it feel to say goodbye to this person? How does it feel to be alone? Take one last look and now your loved one becomes a dot on the horizon and disappears as the clouds surround you. Continue floating.

Now let go of all your worldly thoughts and possessions and worries and relationships. This journey is for you only. Let go of problems in your relationships, your latest work project, your most obsessive worry that you're trying to solve in your life. Let it all go. Feel yourself becoming lighter as you give up these burdens.

Your heavy load is replaced with peace and serenity. Imagine that you feel so light as you leave the cloud that you're floating again. *This time you're floating higher and lighter than before.* Your worries are gone. You're at peace. Experience *you* without those extra burdens. Continue floating and feel free of the heavy load.

You've left the ones you love behind and you've left your problems behind and you're floating through the clouds. How does it feel? How does it feel to be alone without the ones you love and the things that keep you busy or that bog you down? Experience that feeling.

Now in the distance in front of you see a huge altar, a beautiful altar adorned with your favorite colors and precious gems. As you near the altar, stop before it. This is *your* altar. Add anything you want to it. In the center of the altar is a huge life-sized mirror. This magical mirror will enable you to see your *Inner Self*. Not the physical you, but the inner you. That part of you that you've never seen before.

Stand in front of the mirror and see the real you for the first time. *This is your inner self.* Picture your inner self. What does it look like? Who are you really? Is it a small child? Is it a figure in a white robe? Is it a beam of light? Is it an exact replica of you? Or is it a shadowy figure? Really look hard and see it in your mind's eye. Does this self look ashamed, afraid, hurt? Does it have emotional wounds? Is it in pain, sad or angry? Does it have scars from years of mistreatment? Is it crouching out of fear? Or is it standing proudly erect? This is the part of yourself that you have lost touch with because of the details of your outer life.

This is the self you've ignored so that you can take care of everyone and everything else in your life. This is the self-begged for attention and care when you had more important things to do. This is the self you've called worthless and inadequate time and time again. This is the self you've told, "You can't do it." This is the self you've called "stupid" or "dumb" or "unattractive" or in some way put down. This is the self you have scolded for making mistakes. This is the self you've punished with shame and guilt. This is the self you have kicked around all these years, the self you have showered with abuse by overachieving, poor eating habits or lack of rest and exercise. This is the self who has been with you since the day you were born and will be with you until the day you die. This is your best friend. This is the self who stood by you even when you abandoned it. This is the self who has the potential to love you more than anyone on earth. It's time to attend to the wounds of your inner self.

This is the self who longs to be touched, the self who so desperately wants to be loved, accepted and appreciated. This is the self who hasn't received that love because of the walls and barriers built from past hurt. This love, acceptance and appreciation has to begin with you. This is the self who needs your love. It can start here and now.

Step into the mirror and embrace that *inner self*. Feel yourself becoming whole. You already have within you everything you need to make yourself complete. You don't need your work to fill that hole. You don't need other people to make you complete. You don't need anything outside of yourself to be fulfilled. All you need is to be in touch with your *inner self*. The self you're embracing is the self who from now on you'll pay attention to, the one you'll love, care for and affirm. This is the self you'll be there for, the one you'll pamper, the one you'll forgive and allow to make mistakes, the one you'll care for.

Enjoy your own company and be your own best friend. The answers are not in the outside world where you spend most of your time. They are right here within you. As you love yourself fully, all the other problems in your life will solve themselves. You never have to be alone again because you have this *inner* you, that deepest part of you that has always been there and always will be there.

Turn and walk away from the mirror and the altar, carrying your inner self inside of you. Imagine yourself floating again. You're as light as air. Soon you will be going back to the outside world again. The world of computers, rush hours, complex relationships, fast-track living, quick-fixing and stress and burnout. But this time you're not going back empty-handed. You're going back stronger to face the world. You're going back whole, confident and fulfilled. Because you have your *inner self*. See yourself floating through the clouds and slowly back into the room. Imagine yourself coming back into the chair underneath you. Feel the seat beneath you. Feel your feet on the floor. Hear the sounds around you. In any way you want and in your own time, come back to the room. Open your eyes when you are ready.

Affirmations For Your Inner Guru

Self-affirmations help us recognize and appreciate our inner beauty and worth. Sending ourselves balanced, positive affirmations helps us reverse the inner addictive thinking that keeps faulting us as it plays over and over in our minds. Affirming ourselves helps us feel like the smart, capable, and worthy human beings that we truly

are. The following affirmations bring self-acceptance and
inner tranquility:

*My worth doesn't depend on everyone liking me. Things do
not have to be perfect for me to be happy. Life is uncertain, and
people, myself included, are not perfect. I forgive myself for my
imperfections and accept myself just as I am. I am coming to love
and see the beauty within me. I am loving and affirming myself
more and more each day.*

*My happiness comes from within, not without. I do not depend
on the outside world to make me happy. I do not need anything
or anyone, beyond what I already have, to make me happy. I
have everything I need for happiness to fill my life. Wanting
what I have makes me happy and leaves me fulfilled.*

*Today I no longer look for something or someone to make me
feel complete. I am at peace within myself.*

*When I count my blessings, I see that I have much more to be
thankful for than to fret about. Life is full of disappointments,
but I choose to experience them as lessons that build inner forti-
tude and a stronger foundation for my future spiritual growth.*

*I look within myself for answers to my spiritual quest. I know
that through the divine inspiration of my Higher Power spiritual
fulfillment is mine.*

*I do not need another person, my job or material possessions to
make me feel complete. I am whole just as I am. My relationship
to my higher self helps me to feel this wholeness more and more
with each new day.*

*I break the cycle of addictive relationships in my life. My
value as a human being begins with me today through my own
self-acceptance and self-love.*

There are many ways to use these affirmations. You
can write them down and read them to yourself over and

over again. You can record them on tape and play them back or put them up in strategic points around your house. The bathroom mirror is a good location where you'll see the affirmation first thing in the morning.

One of my favorites for the bathroom mirror says,

You are looking at the only person in the world who can determine your happiness.

Keep a bulletin board with all the affirming notes, gifts and sayings that people send you. Look at them often to remind yourself that others see you as a wonderful human being. You can make up your own affirmations that give you confidence to surmount a particular problem in your life. You can keep a special notebook or journal of your own created affirmations or those you've found in other places. If you have an answering machine on your telephone, you can call yourself from work or another location and leave affirming messages. It's a wonderful experience to come home from a hard day and hear a loving and affirming message for yourself just as if it were from someone else who cares as much about you.

Connecting With Your Inner Guru

When we live our lives to the fullest, we live our lives for ourselves, not for others. We do not allow the insignificant day-to-day trifles to detract from the truly important things in our lives. And we live our lives so that we will never have any regrets. Each of us is unique. No one will ever experience life in exactly the same way we do. No one else will see and feel about things exactly the same. No one will have the identical experiences that are filtered through our brain in the exact same way. No one else will talk to the same people at the exact split moment. No one will enjoy the same interchange of humor or see the way the light angles off a loved one's face or watch the evening rain clouds roll in behind a silhouetted sunset. No one but us.

Each breath we take is exclusively ours. No one else will breathe through these lungs, see through these eyes, hear through these ears or feel with these hands and heart. No one else will have the same chance to help another person who needs help at that instant and to teach the people who need to learn something at that second. What splendid creatures we are! How lucky we are to have this once-in-a-lifetime chance to live our lives in our own unique way!

I challenge you to affirm and love yourself. Be yourself. Pamper yourself. Forgive and care for yourself. Enjoy your own company and be your own best friend. Do the things for you that you would do for the ones you love the most. And you will heal.

Our healing eyes show us how to put a strong fence around the top of the cliff instead of an ambulance down in the valley. Recovery from addictive thinking teaches us that we no longer have to jump off a ledge into the Grand Canyon to enjoy its beauty. We can stand by the edge and let our hearts do the soaring for us.

FURTHER READING

Becker, Robert. (1989). **Addicted To Misery: The Other Side Of Co-dependency.** Deerfield Beach, FL: Health Communications.

Burns, David. (1980). **Feeling Good: The New Mood Therapy.** New York: The New American Library.

Capra, Fritjof. (1984). **The Tao Of Physics.** New York. Bantam.

Cousins, Norman. (1989). **Headfirst: The Biology Of Hope.** New York: E.P. Dutton.

DeMello, Anthony. (1985). **Wellsprings: A Book Of Spiritual Exercises.** New York: Doubleday.

Dyer, Wayne. (1989). **You'll See It When You Believe It.** New York: William Morrow and Company.

Ellis, Albert and Robert Harper. (1975). **A New Guide To Rational Living.** Hollywood, CA: Wilshire Book Company.

Fishel, Ruth. (1991). **Healing Energy: The Power Of Recovery.** Deerfield Beach, FL: Health Communications.

Frankl, Viktor. (1959). **Man's Search For Meaning.** New York: Washington Square Press.

Gawain, Shakti. (1978). **Creative Visualization.** Mill Valley, CA: Whatever Publishing.

Hay, Louise. (1984). **You Can Heal Your Life.** Santa Monica, CA: Hay House.

Houff, William. (1989). **Infinity In Your Hand.** Spokane, WA: Melior Publications.

Keyes, Ken. (1975). **Handbook Of Higher Consciousness.** St. Mary, KY: Living Love Publications.

MacLaine, Shirley. (1989). **Going Within: A Guide For Inner Transformation.** New York: Bantam.

Miller, Joy. (1989). **Addictive Relationships: Reclaiming Your Boundaries.** Deerfield Beach, FL: Health Communications.

Murphy, Joseph. (1968). **The Cosmic Power Within You.** West Nyack, New York: Parker Publishers.

Ponder, Catherine. (1962). **The Dynamic Laws Of Prosperity.** Englewood Cliffs, NJ: Prentice-Hall.

Robinson, Bryan. (1989). **Work Addiction: Hidden Legacies Of Adult Children.** Deerfield Beach, FL: Health Communications.

Robinson, Bryan. (1989). **Working With Children Of Alcoholics: The Practitioners Handbook.** Lexington, MA: Lexington Books.

Robinson, Bryan. (1990). **Soothing Moments: Daily Meditations For Fast-Track Living.** Deerfield Beach, FL: Health Communications.

Robinson, Bryan. (1991). **Healograms: Healing Messages For Co-dependents.** Deerfield Beach, FL: Health Communications.

Siegel, Bernie. (1986). **Love, Medicine & Miracles.** New York: Harper & Row.

Valles, Carlos. (1988). **Mastering Sadhana.** New York: Doubleday.

Wills-Brandon, Carla. (1990). **Learning To Say No: Establishing Healthy Boundaries.** Deerfield Beach, FL: Health Communications.

Wing, R.L. (1986). **The Tao Of Power.** New York: Doubleday.

Zukav, Gary. (1989). The Seat Of The Soul. New York: Simon & Schuster.

New Books . . .
from Health Communications

ALTERNATIVE PATHWAYS TO HEALING: The Recovery Medicine Wheel
Kip Coggins, MSW
This book with its unique approach to recovery explains the concept of the medicine wheel — and how you can learn to live in harmony with yourself, with others and with the earth.
ISBN 1-55874-089-9   **$7.95**

UNDERSTANDING CO-DEPENDENCY
Sharon Wegscheider-Cruse, M.A., and Joseph R. Cruse, M.D.
The authors give us a basic understanding of co-dependency that everyone can use — what it is, how it happens, who is affected by it and what can be done for them.
ISBN 1-55874-077-5   **$7.95**

THE OTHER SIDE OF THE FAMILY:
A Book For Recovery From Abuse, Incest And Neglect
Ellen Ratner, Ed.M.
This workbook addresses the issues of the survivor — self-esteem, feelings, defenses, grieving, relationships and sexuality — and goes beyond to help them through the healing process.
ISBN 1-55874-110-0   **$13.95**

OVERCOMING PERFECTIONISM:
The Key To A Balanced Recovery
Ann W. Smith, M.S.
This book offers practical hints, together with a few lighthearted ones, as a guide toward learning to "live in the middle." It invites you to let go of your superhuman syndrome and find a balanced recovery.
ISBN 1-55874-111-9   **$8.95**

LEARNING TO SAY NO:
Establishing Healthy Boundaries
Carla Wills-Brandon, M.A.
If you grew up in a dysfunctional family, establishing boundaries is a difficult and risky decision. Where do you draw the line? Learn to recognize yourself as an individual who has the power to say no.
ISBN 1-55874-087-2   **$8.95**

3201 S.W. 15th Street,
Deerfield Beach, FL 33442-8190
1-800-851-9100

Health
Communications, Inc.

Daily Affirmation Books from . . .
Health Communications

GENTLE REMINDERS FOR CO-DEPENDENTS: *Daily Affirmations*
Mitzi Chandler

With insight and humor, Mitzi Chandler takes the co-dependent and the adult child through the year. Gentle Reminders is for those in recovery who seek to enjoy the miracle each day brings.

ISBN 1-55874-020-1 $6.95

TIME FOR JOY: *Daily Affirmations*
Ruth Fishel

With quotations, thoughts and healing energizing affirmations these daily messages address the fears and imperfections of being human, guiding us through self-acceptance to a tangible peace and the place within where there is *time for joy.*

ISBN 0-932194-82-6 $6.95

AFFIRMATIONS FOR THE INNER CHILD
Rokelle Lerner

This book contains powerful messages and helpful suggestions aimed at adults who have unfinished childhood issues. By reading it daily we can end the cycle of suffering and move from pain into recovery.

ISBN 1-55874-045-6 $6.95

DAILY AFFIRMATIONS: *For Adult Children of Alcoholics*
Rokelle Lerner

Affirmations are a way to discover personal awareness, growth and spiritual potential, and self-regard. Reading this book gives us an opportunity to nurture ourselves, learn who we are and what we want to become.

ISBN 0-932194-47-3
(Little Red Book) $6.95
(New Cover Edition) $6.95

SOOTHING MOMENTS: *Daily Meditations For Fast-Track Living*
Bryan E. Robinson, Ph.D.

This is designed for those leading fast-paced and high-pressured lives who need time out each day to bring self-renewal, joy and serenity into their lives.

ISBN 1-55874-075-9 $6.95

3201 S.W. 15th Street,
Deerfield Beach, FL 33442-8190
1-800-851-9100

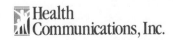
Health
Communications, Inc.